Saturday Dogs

...and the owners they trained

Susan Overfield

Susan Overfield

MUDDY
CREEK
PUBLISHING

Published in the United States by Muddy Creek Publishing
PO Box 556, Vaughn MT 59487   mcp@3riversdbs.net
http://www.muddycreekpublishing.com

Muddy Creek Publishing and its logo are registered
trademarks.
Book cover design by Matt Hocevar
Interior design by Brenden Koch

Library of Congress Cataloging-in-Publication Data
Library of Congress Control Number: 2007910062
Overfield, Susan.
Saturday Dogs...and the owners they trained / Susan Overfield
p.   cm.
ISBN 0-980-2199-5-7

Printed in Canada
First Edition / First Printing

The Trilogy of Dedication:

With much love, respect and admiration to
The Man – Ric
The Friend – Pam
The Dog – Newt

Without all three this would
never have been possible.

TABLE OF CONTENTS

His Finest Hour

Guess Who's Coming to Dinner

Terrorist Cell

Group Therapy

Acknowledgements

Introduction

"You should write a book." I have heard that so often I couldn't even hazard a guess as to how many times. I dismissed it each and every time.

The problem was that I was being told to write about my training method. You can't learn to train dogs from a book unless you already know how to train dogs. Books, videos, television shows...they can't correct your timing, your intensity, or your tone. They can't answer questions or build your confidence or tell you if your gut feeling about what you think your dog is doing and feeling is right or wrong. They can only give you one more idea about how to train a dog and then let you go and screw it up. Then you're frustrated and both you and the dog stop trying. It's a no-win situation.

Through all the years I've worked dogs I've learned quite a bit. I had to acknowledge that my emotional state was every bit as important as how much I knew and how well I handled dogs. It gave me a unique perspective on what was wrong in the majority of training methods and the trainers that taught them. I found insight into the average dog owners, their insecurities, and what they were communicating to their dog.

I watched owners become embarrassed, be looked down upon, judged for handling abilities, and carry so much stress that it was misery for their dogs. It then turned into a misery and self-condemnation and loss of confidence for the owner.

It became extremely important to me that the average dog owner not have that experience if I could help it.

I learned that some owners will never want their dogs to have a good life if it means they must give up their own emotional bad habits, say no to their dogs or be a leader; stop remembering the dog as a victim, realize that the dog is not their child or spouse, and insist on good manners from their dog, with all that encompasses.

Others, however, really wanted what was best for the dog they loved; they simply didn't know what was true, what wasn't. They didn't know what worked, what didn't and how to achieve good behavior.

Most trainers didn't know, either. They were really no help at all to people. They held to old ways, cost owners loads of money, destroyed confidence, increased frustration and could never explain dogs. It was simply, "do it this way", regardless or not if it was the way dogs did it, understood it, or if they could explain why it worked or didn't to the owner. But, they write loads of books. So do the dog behaviorists.

Funny thing, dogs don't read books.

We can generalize all we want about dogs, indicators of behavior, response, training and learning, and while some of that is true and can be used, what isn't in the equation is the gross environmental changes we've forced on our companions and the individual dog. Without knowledge of those two factors, you can't train—or train easily and well. Since the dogs aren't reading the books, they don't follow the generalized outline as explained by trainers and behaviorists. Then owners don't get the response they think they should, or the owner doesn't know what to do when the dog doesn't respond in the popularly identified manner and it's a downhill spiral from there.

The other hitch in the equation was the scientific community filled with professionals who all studied the dog and its behavior and then wrote about it. Some of what they penned was interesting, but far from new or unknown by those who actually were down in the trenches with the dogs. Some was interesting as it was new in the sense that it was tracked information which substantiated successfully implemented methods by "unconventional" or non-traditional method trainers.

The largest lack, however, in the dog training industry, is the decided absence of consilient thinking. Over the millennia that dogs have been at the side of humans, our decisions and abilities to alter our environment have created great distances between nature and human. We have creatively and competently restructured our "world" to work for humans. Our brains have envisioned, and our will and bodies have created a different environment from that in which our ancestors were genetically predisposed to function. In many ways we have made our lives easier, more efficient, and less costly as regards to health, welfare and mortality issues. Throughout all the changes the dog has been along for the ride, but had no part in the environmental restructuring, and so has had no reason to truly adapt to the same extent as we humans.

We forget this. The dog industry doesn't even know it. I liken it to humans having entered a house in which the door is the portal between nature and our created world. We stand on the inside; the dog is still out on nature's porch. The dog is still much closer to nature in all its forms and functions, and we are not meeting its needs.

A successful training method which incorporates, acknowledges and adapts to the dog, which is still in touch with the nature portion of its behavior and responses that humans have lost touch with, is rarely used within the dog training industry. It is considered a quack method by mainstream training standards, yet the proof speaks for itself. It has consistently high success rates and long-term stability within the behavioral, psychological, emotional and social parameters of the dog.

Then, suddenly, one day it dawned on me that what needed to be written was a book that showed owners a reflection of themselves. If they could see themselves, see what had been changed in the story and then go on to an analysis and explanation of the dog, the owner, the behavior and the responses by both, they might have an easier time making those changes in themselves. It might open the door for specific questions from them, different responses and an opportunity to see their dog differently.

Then all the dogs I have worked over the many years came back to me and the book was suddenly real.

This, then, is the outcome. It is for every dog that ever trained its owner.

Susan Overfield
September 2007

Chapter 1

In the Beginning was "Aaahtt"

Saturday morning. No wind, which in itself is a miracle in Montana; and it would be a hot day. In front of me stood eight people, eight dogs, sixteen stories and a thousand excuses. The world couldn't produce enough coffee to prepare me for some of the Saturday classes.

The owners had called me in order to sign-up for behavioral obedience. The commencement of the conversations never varied. "I was referred to you. I have a dog..." The tone, however, spoke volumes: harried, frustrated, defensive, confused, embarrassed or cautiously hopeful—a myriad of emotions, offering a glimpse of the individual and allowing me to begin building a mental picture of the real problem. Rarely did what the owners recount in the way of their dogs' behavioral and obedience issues coincide with the reality of the problem or cause.

"What breed of dog?" I'd squeeze this question in at the first break for breath by the client, followed rapidly with, "How old is the dog?" in order to forestall any further possibility of a long, rambling anecdote.

"A Yorkie...six months..."

"A Lab...three years..."

"A golden retriever...a year old..."

"A Border collie...six..."

I'd jump in and happily list all the behavioral problems facing the owner. I was not often wrong or far-off the mark. The telephone assessment was usually greeted with a gasp of astonishment as if I'd offered a psychic reading, "Yes, that's exactly what he's doing."

"Not a problem, bring him along this Saturday. We'll fix it." Tendrils of unspoken disbelief, or renewed hope, seeped through the phone line.

Once upon a time I sat patiently while the person chronicled the pup's antics, the youthful indiscretions of an adolescent dog, or of a previous, horrible life from which the dog was saved. As more and more dogs came to me with problems, I jettisoned that habit and quickly took control of the conversations and owners in the same manner I quickly took control of their dogs. It was better for everyone.

Now I stood facing a mixed-bag group of dogs spanning all ages, from a mere pup of eight weeks to a veteran of misbehavior at age six. Some of the people had been coming to class for a short time and some were almost at the end of the sessions, as I offer fluid training, (that is as one client and dog finish their set of sessions and "graduate" another duo is admitted to class. I constantly have a changing group of dogs, owners, and competency levels.) But the new people stood tense and embarrassed and I could read their thoughts as they prayed silently that it wouldn't be their dog which would be the worst in the group. One or two sighed almost audibly with happiness to observe a nearby dog whose behavior was actually worse than theirs and you could see them visibly relax.

"I have no tact. I'm not picking on you, but if I see you or your dog doing something that needs correcting I'll point it out, because other people will run up against the same thing at some time. I'm unconventional. I want you to forget everything you've ever read, seen, or heard about dog training. It was all set up for humans, by humans. You need to learn how dogs deal with dogs. I don't want you to repeat a command; you say it once and only once. You'll learn a correction sound that all dogs understand. Dogs comply with this method in about ten minutes; you may take hours to grasp it." At this moment a late arrival appeared and parked. I watched in astonishment as the car began to rock back and forth. What in God's name was in there? An elephant?

As the vehicle idled the driver's door opened an infinitesimal crack and a young woman slid out. Keeping one hand inside the car she hurriedly pushed the door closed, removing her fingers at the last possible moment. Hair jumbled, a large wet spot on her shoulder, her face displayed strain as she walked toward me looking repeatedly over her shoulder at the shuddering car. "I'm Kathy Hammond and I called you about my dog."

"Right...well, bring him over."

"I can't get him out of the car alone."

Odd, I thought, what kind of dog was it that she couldn't remove from a car? Stealing a glance at the bouncing car I couldn't discern a thing in the dark interior.

"Okay, I'll help." We headed for the car and I asked, "Why don't you shut it down and we'll get him out?"

"Oh, no, if the car's running he's willing to stay inside. If I shut it off he'll get out." There was real fear in her voice.

The car's rocking increased as we approached. Suddenly the driver's entire window was filled with a black head the size of a small tire, two large, golden eyes shining with eagerness and a wet, pink tongue that rolled out, bringing to mind the red carpet leading to Air Force One. This impression was backed up by a sound ominously emanating from the inside that was uncomfortably reminiscent of a jumbo jet's engines on high idle.

The dog's uninhibited excitement sent the car's motion into high gear. I could only think of the rather stupid little rhyme I'd often heard, "If the car's rockin', don't come knockin'." Suddenly, it sounded very apt.

"What breed is he?"

"A Lab," her voice quavered as she tried to control her tears.

I relaxed - Labs weren't geared to eat people, so we had that on our side. "Hey, don't cry, we'll take care of it. Getting upset won't help him."

"I can't control him, he's too big. He drags me everywhere, and when he sees these other dogs he'll make right for them and I won't be able to stop him." Here it was in a nut-shell: the fear, lack of confidence, embarrassment, defeat, all communicated to her dog, which ensured he would take the helm in this relationship. Empowerment squared.

I just didn't get it, he was a Lab. Yes, they can be strong, and their pulling could keep us off-balance and make controlling and walking them difficult, but he was a Lab. Labs average seventy pounds.

"Does he have a leash on?"

"Yes."

"Then here is what we'll do," I assured her confidently "Open the door, grab his leash, and I'll slip mine over his head. That way there'll be two of us hanging on and we'll be able to control him. That will let you turn off the car and then we'll head over to the group."

She looked at me as if I'd lost my mind, but inched the door open. The car shuddered violently and the next thing I knew the dog bulled his way past her in his desire to meet me, the new thing on the block.

My reaction came from years of practice at catching out-of-control dogs. My leash fell neatly over his head, as I mentally acknowledged that the choke chain he was wearing didn't have any effect on his behavior, and then I suffered whiplash. With both of us hanging on for dear life, digging feet into the gravel of the drive, Kathy and I were propelled forward by a force of nature. Out of the corner of my eye I glimpsed the other dogs and people in the class go dead still in shock.

This was NOT a Lab. This was not

TWO Labs. This was a black hole in the universe—energy sucking everything near it into the vortex of hyper-activity. One-hundred-thirty-eight pounds of one-and-a-half-year old dog, with not a thought in his head but to move forward and greet all living things, and my place offered a buffet of creatures to satisfy his congenial appetite: sheep, dogs, cats, horses, the neighboring cattle, and forty acres to explore in case he'd missed anything. We were on a dry-ground, Nantucket sleigh ride.

"Aahhtt!!" The correction sound, that in ninety-nine percent of the cases I've encountered stopped a dog in his tracks, failed to elicit any response from the behemoth intent on reaching the group in front of us.

The small knot of dogs that had once been yipping, tugging, squirming, investigating the ground in front of them, waiting quietly, or wagging tails, all wore a panicked look as the correction sound sunk into their collective psyche. They instantly wanted to comply, while simultaneously they observed the on-coming freight train, fondly called "Brand", and wanted to flee before the wreck reached them. Their owners, slower to understand what was happening, displayed a growing look of horror as they watched this Baskervillian canine, seemingly without effort, drag the collective two-hundred-plus pounds of resisting females inexorably toward them. As we slid by my rail fence, I threw myself to the side and dug in, wrapping the leash around the post. Brand's body ceased its forward motion, but his intent never wavered as he continued to try to reach the other dogs that now sat dumbstruck against owners that were frozen in place.

Quivering with exertion, after our less-than-controlled entrance into class, I looped the leash around the top of the post, dodging the cudgel of a tail, which was swinging wildly in all directions, I went to stand by Kathy. Practically in tears, apologizing to everyone, she was the perfect picture of abject misery.

"Kathy, stop." I took the leash from her, unclipped it from the choke collar, and looped it over Brand's head, then handed the end back to her. "This is your window of opportunity to take charge and change everything. All you need to do today is insist he sit, calm down, and stay seated. He's anchored to the post, so you'll be fine." I moved back to the center of the dogs and began class.

By the end of two hours Brand had calmed considerably. So much in fact, that Kathy was able to walk him to the car alone without any pulling. He sat upon command at the car door and waited until he was told to get in. It was the first time in almost fourteen months that Kathy had enough control over him to be able to walk anywhere on a leash. Her confidence took a mighty jump. I could tell it would be a good week for her and Brand.

The second Saturday for Kathy and Brand had a bite to the air; autumn would begin in a couple of weeks. The dogs were in high spirits with the cooler temperature and the people unloading their dogs were brief summaries of how much they had improved their abilities with their dogs.

"Wait, take that dog back, put it in the car again, and insist that it wait calmly until you tell it to get out. Then make it walk to the group in a polite manner," I yelled across the intervening pasture to a man whose dog had charged out of the back of his vehicle.

I took a keen interest when I saw Kathy emerge from her car. The signs were good, the car was immobile. Everything seemed to be going well. Brand got out of the car calmly, sat, and waited for Kathy to tell him to walk.

As they began to make their way toward us, I watched Brand begin to build up excitement and increase speed. Kathy corrected, but Brand had, once again, put his one working brain cell on hold. I went to help her and we took Brand back to her car.

"Make him sit here and calm down

before you try again," I counseled, "and every time he starts to get out of hand, return to the car and begin again. He needs to learn that the only way he'll get something he wants is if his behavior is calm."

It took five attempts before Brand realized that he could not join the other dogs if he continued behaving the way he did. I kept watching him while I spoke to the group which stood around me in a semi-circle relating the events of the past week, good and bad, and questioning me as to whether they handled it well or not.

Brand was so massive that all he did was on a grand scale. His food intake was impressive; his affection was in the great dramatic actions of the quintessential ham actor; and what he lacked in speed, he made up for in sound, gasping and emitting an amusing "humph" noise as he pounded the earth in an ungainly run. He was not an athlete. And so, when he experienced his epiphany, it was large and easy to read. You could actually see the dawning of the concept, "If I don't walk nicely and behave, I won't get to be with the other dogs." It was as if he threw a self-control switch, and he struggled not to pull as they finally came to class.

Upon entering the "inner circle," Brand sat with great pride and quivered with adrenaline, which he was barely managing to control, as he took stock of the dogs around him. Kathy was slightly out of breath, but she, too, was proud.

I handed out the various exercises for the day, pairing some of the more experienced owners, who had been in class longer, with the newer people. I found that this helped everyone involved, as the more advanced dog/owner combinations shared trials, tribulations, and successes, as well as knowledge and skill, with the novice handler. The more advanced "student" benefited by having to review, mentally, information he had learned, and the new "student" benefited from hearing the horror stories. It gave them hope, as tales were recounted with gusto of wrecks, and near-wrecks, and how dog and owner had survived and improved.

Also, there were times some people simply didn't have the confidence to question me about how or why we did something. Or, they felt they weren't "getting it", and had asked too often a question about the same problem. Pairing the advanced with the novice allowed the inexperienced to ask the question again of a peer. The more advanced owner, usually, had built enough confidence to voice the question in a group setting while we took a break in work. It taught all levels of owners that questions are good and should be asked. It aided all the newer students in reaching a more relaxed and comfortable level within the class as they came to realize that they'd not be judged for asking any questions or repeatedly asking the same question until they understood. The benefits were enormous, and as owner confidence and ease increased, it was reflected in the behavior of the dog.

"Kath, you'll walk Brand today." Her face blanched and her confidence nosedived. "What is that look? Stop it. You can do this," I insisted.

"He'll pull, and then get away from me," she almost wailed.

I moderated my tone. "Brand can learn to walk nicely without popping, choking, or disciplining, in ten minutes or less, I promise. Traditional classes may take an hour or more of instructions, and then expect you to go home and practice walking, but it's not needed. Ask anyone in class."

Heads nodded in affirmation and one person spoke up, "She's right. I didn't think I could do it, but Jazz stopped pulling after just a few minutes, and walks are great now."

Letting the others loose to work on their assignments, I stayed back to help Kathy with Brand. Within a short time she was positively glowing with joy as she and Brand walked the property without a hitch. At the end of class she returned to the group and burst out, "I thought he was going to try to chase the sheep and pull me over, but I gave the correction sound, made him get calm, and then we continued walking. We didn't have a problem!"

From that point onward Kathy and Brand sailed through every exercise they were given. In the third class, when told to drop the leash and walk with Brand, she had a moment's hesitation, but overcame that quickly and took command, successfully navigating the other dogs and livestock without a problem. By the fifth and final class, Kathy never even put a leash on Brand as they got out of the car and joined the group. A small, quiet correction was all that was needed to remind this once out-of-control dog of what was expected in the way of behavior; and he instantly self-corrected, and life went on happily.

Kathy and Brand finished their classes and, in the end, Kathy could not only walk Brand on-leash, but could safely and confidently allow him to be off-leash as well—any place, at any time. He calmed down, listened to and respected Kathy, and their relationship blossomed. Kathy's husband was transferred out-of-state and I only heard from them once more. They were living where Brand had acres of room to run and play, but Kathy assured me he still listened and was very well-behaved.

"He's the best dog I've ever had, and I didn't think I'd ever say that about him." These words, proudly said, were the last I heard from her.

Brand, Labrador retriever, age 18 months

Brand's symptoms were numerous: barking, excitement, jumping, not coming when called, didn't hold a sit/stay, was unable to walk nicely on a leash. The problem was simple: the owner wasn't respected as the leader, she received no respect from the dog and could not enforce her commands. As a pup, Brand's exuberance was greeted with physical affection by humans and out-of-control behavior was excused away saying he was only a puppy. His training had begun, but it was all wrong.

Humans confuse the excitement, jumping and licking of their faces as an expression of excitement to see them, which is correct, and of love, which is incorrect. The licking is an atavistic response to a returning leader and, in the wild, would cause regurgitation of food collected by their mother, or other older dogs, for the pups' consumption. Of course they're excited; the dinner bell rings with the returning dogs. I believe that allowing this form of behavior to continue for long will, in effect, cause a form of behavioral immaturity, freezing the pups' emotional and mental development at a specific point. It also teaches the dog that jumping, licking, and hyper-activity are condoned and rewarded in the "pack" in which they live.

While this might not be a problem

when the pup is a mere fifteen pounds, it is catastrophic when the dog reaches sixty, or in this case, one-hundred thirty-eight pounds. The fact that Brand believed that a hyperactive, out-of-control greeting was acceptable pointed to the fact that his owner had failed where dogs would have succeeded. Dogs in an established group would have taught, very quickly, the proper etiquette for meeting and greeting another dog.

In the majority of obedience training the initial class teaches the dog to walk on a leash properly. A choke chain or treat is used to enforce the desired command. Choke chains are a human invention, created to help humans gain mastery over the dog. Dogs don't need them, unless the human is incapable, or unwilling, to master good communication, which unequivocally states "I'm in charge and we do it my way."

Over forty-five years ago it was established that painful stimuli intercepted middle-cortex learning and focused the thought pattern on the stimuli, not the action. Choke chains teach what is termed "learned helplessness." Don't try anything or it may hurt. This results in a dog which must be given commands to function. The choke chain must be looked at as a tool to be discarded as quickly as possible once the HUMAN has learned how to communicate with the dog. Too often it is an over-used

16

braking system that becomes a necessity for life as the humans haven't been taught to communicate with their dog.

Here we had a dog which was totally oblivious to the purpose of the choke chain and continued pell-mell, wheezing and gasping, toward the object of its desire. Kathy had no control, and the choke chain was ineffective. She repeatedly called Brand's name and gave a variety of commands: no, sit, stay and come. They rolled off his back with no effect whatsoever.

My first goal, in this impending disaster scenario, was to stop Brand from continuing forward. A moving dog, in the initial phase of training, thinks only one thing: "...keep moving until I reach my goal." I often tell my clients, "Body in motion, brain in neutral." This is one reason why EVERY time I begin training a dog we do NOT start with the walk, we work on ONLY a sit—for two solid hours.

By insisting the dog sit, and enforcing that command, a variety of issues are dealt with simultaneously and successfully. The dog learns to respect the "Aahht," which is a correction sound indicating that the current exhibited behavior is unacceptable; self-correcting, and returning to a sit ensures no further discipline from the owner. The dog also is kicking its thinking into gear as it must "problem solve" and decide what it is the owner is requiring when it hears "Aahht." Expending all this mental energy helps calm the dog and make it more manageable.

The owner is not faced with attempting to learn and master a new skill, such as on-leash walking, while physically fighting the hyper-active dog and probably losing the battle. If the ultimate goal is to instruct the dog not to challenge the owner's commands, but instead to obey them, why would any training method want to begin by letting the dog learn to challenge the owner and then win the battle of the walk and drag the owner around? This, simply stated, teaches the dog the owner's weakness and empowers the dog to challenge harder, thus taking an inordinately long time to teach the desired behavior.

In my class the owner has one issue, and only one issue, to deal with in the beginning: enforcing the command to sit. The owner can then begin to relax as he experiences a small success. It also enables him to concentrate on what I'm telling him about dogs, their behavior, why they act and react the way they do, what motivates the dog, how and when to effectively correct misbehavior, and creates an opportunity for the owner to ask questions.

I assign each dog and owner a specific exercise to accomplish during each class. No two dogs are the same and the exercises reflect that by being tailored to the individual duo. In traditional training, be it with a choke chain or a positive/treat method, the trainer has a set number of dogs and owners to deal with for the entire time the classes are set to run. This conditions the dog to obey with that group only, and the owner is then faced with the wide world, and the problems the dog still evidences in greeting new people and animals. It also, unintentionally, pits owners against each other for the award, actual or perceived, of the "best dog" in class. This undermines the confidence of many owners as the sessions progress and that lack of confidence is transmitted to the dog (which then begins to ignore the owner). By creating a fluid training class, the dogs learn the skill of meeting new people and dogs as they constantly come and go in the course of classes. The owner is taught how to deal with this real-life situation in class where help can be had and bad behavior stopped, not thrown on the streets without support or back-up. The owners appreciate it, and the dogs are better for it.

At the end of the first class the owner has gained some confidence in his control of the dog, and the dog has gained some respect for the owner's ability to enforce a simple command. They are sent home to work on one thing, their dog holding a sit whenever, and wherever, they command it. They never fail to return the second week pleased and surprised that the immediate, overall change they saw in their dog in the first class has held and improved, as has their ability to control and direct the dog's behavior.

Both are now well on their way to a successful relationship in which the dog thinks and the owner is a competent leader and partner. Both are much happier.

Questions and Answers

Q: My dog doesn't walk nicely on a leash, so why spend the first class insisting that it sit and not work on the real problem? And why am I supposed to change how I act and change what I do? Why discipline with your "word"? Why not praise him with a pat, or treat, when he does well?

A: I try to teach humans how dogs teach dogs. Nature and the dog developed this method, they understand it, they learn it easily, and they teach it well to new dogs. Dogs don't use treats, they don't pet each other, and the first thing they learn is how to be calm and polite around others. I believe, since our dogs will never behave like a person, it is our responsibility as humans to do the changing in order to give the dog an opportunity to shine.

The dog must sit in order to begin learning to be patient, calm, think, and to respect the fact you told it to sit and, therefore, it must follow the command. If it ignores your command, you will correct its behavior. It is so much easier to correct for a sit than to correct a dog that's pulling, jumping, barking, and lunging at everything in its path. You will be too exhausted to continue to insist on a change in a behavior and will become frustrated and stop trying. You will have also begun to instruct the dog to challenge your commands and continue to challenge until you give up. I'm geared for success, for both dog and owner, and I believe this to be the most basic of behavioral instruction which establishes the owner as the leader and capable of enforcing the rules.

I believe in discipline, making the dog mind and doing what I want. Because I'm ultimately responsible for the dog and the impression it makes, I have certain expectations of behavior and the responsibility of teaching social skills. My pup has been removed from its biological mother who would have taught all the necessary survival and social skills and I must take up that mantle of instruction for the overall, well-being of my dog. I must ensure my dogs' safety, social capabilities, and good manners. To do this I must clearly communicate to my dogs what I expect. They must understand what happens when they follow the rules and when they ignore them. They MUST respect me in order for us to develop a safe, harmonious, loving relationship which fosters individuality for each dog without sacrificing the overall well-being of the "pack."

I take the long-range view when training or raising dogs. A pup's behavior at 20 pounds may be cute to some, but when the dog is 90 pounds it's not—it may even be dangerous. If the average life expectancy for a dog is 12 years, why would I want almost half of that to be lived by the dog in insecurity and confusion? Those first six years are being wasted while the dog teaches itself how to fit into the family and ages to a point where it doesn't try new things at every opportunity. My dog should not suffer because I am unwilling to do the one thing which could make life easier for him, and that is to communicate clearly what it is I expect in the way of behavior.

I love my dogs, and grieve deeply when I lose one. But I would be remiss, and a failure as an owner, just as I would be a failure to my children, if I allowed them to do as they please simply because it made them happy. Love is built over time. It's tested, tried and survives if the foundation is there and true. I cannot take a short-term view for momentary happiness if it sacrifices long-term goals of acceptance, trust, safety, and love for, and from, my dogs.

My dogs, your dogs, dogs in shelters, dogs on the street, and dogs in India are just that dogs. They are hard-wired from birth to be dogs. Not elephants, not humans, not children—just dogs. We must deal with them as dogs or run the risk of making them disliked, psychotic, and neurotic in their attempts to understand what we humans want from them. To allow them to do as they please, without establishing clear, concise, behavior rules that you, as leader, enforce, does not make them happy, but insecure, stressed, and worried. If love really is the cure-all, then why do so many people pay so much money to fix bad behavior and habits? Why are so many dogs dumped, ignored, or euthanized? It should be enough that you love your dog and that will cause it to behave perfectly. It doesn't work that way, and the sooner humans see the truth, learn to do it correctly, the way nature has hard-wired dogs to learn, the sooner the dogs will benefit.

Dogs require social structure, a firm knowledge of behavioral expectations within their pack, skills to interact with the world at large, and clear delineation of right and wrong and the consequences of breaking rules, before they can form emotional attachments. They need clear, strong leaders to monitor the pack, maintain peace, and teach rules, supply food, affection and discipline. They relax when these things are in place. They form a deeper attachment to the human which supplies this structure.

They trust, they behave, they love, they enjoy, and they receive all this in return on a much deeper, atavistic level than mere treat/bribes and pats on the head can impart. When in doubt, the dog will look to the human, if it's the leader, for a cue on how to behave in new situations.

Without all this, the dog will take charge. He will become increasingly frustrated because the humans aren't following the rules he, the dog, lays down as the leader, and he will react as the dog he is. The problem with this is that the way a dog would discipline or behave, is not always acceptable within the human framework. Biting may be an acceptable disciplinary action amongst dogs, but humans take a very dim view of it.

I have heard countless times from people who trained dogs utilizing traditional methods, and then trained a dog the way I teach, state they would never train any other way, that this dog was their best dog. That they totally trusted the dog, could allow it more freedom because they could trust it, and that they really liked the dog. They didn't worry about what it would do around new people, new dogs, or in new situations. They knew they could trust it to behave and mind. Because of this, the dog was included in their lives more fully, taken more places, involved in more social situations, trusted in off-leash and out-of-yard environments. The people were more aware of their dog's needs and were capable of meeting them. The dog, in return, was more than willing to follow the rules. The dogs received constant reaffirmation that their behavior was good, they were good, and their humans loved them. In short, both the owners and dogs had a deeper, more satisfying relationship.

ALL animals have certain acceptable and unacceptable behavior within their groupings which they are taught to recognize. Humans have it—people have rules within their families, religions, communities, and cultures. If we break the rules ignorance is not acceptable, we pay the consequences. We dislike people who consistently ignore rules and make life difficult for the rest of us. We insist they be "punished" for their misbehavior, whether we do it personally, or legally. Dogs are no different and quickly impart rules to newcomers or developing pups. So, why is it that many humans loathe to set rules for their dogs?

A study, completed by Tufts University, determined "that owners of dogs with behavioral problems generally scored lower on the personality test (California Personality Inventory/CPI), and, more specifically, on the particular personality scales concerned with measuring confidence, independence, dominance and sociability. Owners of dogs with a behavior problem scored less favorably on 20 of the 23 personality scales measured...In particular, the findings indicate that more confident, independent-minded persons are less likely to be confronted with a canine behavior problem...owners of aggressive dogs tend to be "tense, emotionally less stable, shy, and undisciplined,""...('Comparison of Personality Inventories of Owners of Dogs With and Without Behavior Problems', Dodman, BVMS, DACVB, et al., 2002)

The long and the short of this study is that what the owner feels, and thus communicates to the dog in the way of his own self-confidence and abilities to lead in any situation, has a direct affect and effect on the dog's behavior.

The study also discussed the owners who engaged in anthropomorphic relationships (assigning human attributes) with their dogs. By treating the dogs as human the owners actually created many behavioral problems such as hyper-activity, fighting, insecurity and neurotic responses.

So, if making my (or anyone's) dogs' lives easier because they are secure in the knowledge of what's expected of them, if including them more fully in my life, if allowing them more personal freedom because I can trust them, if communicating my emotional pleasure and contentment of their presence, if the positive emotional response to their good behavior each time they greet ncw pcoplc is a dircct rcsult of my insisting they follow rules or there will be discipline, if you consider this to be mean or wrong, if you consider what I teach harsh or lacking in love, then I must say I will NOT change as the bottom line is the dogs. I cannot change the opinions or behavior of humans who do not wish to change. I can only do my best to give each dog what it needs most to be the best dog it can be. I will continue to try to help others do the same in order that they may enjoy a deeper relationship, trust, and understanding with their dog.

Chapter  2

"... An Escape from Emotion ..."

Eliot

"I have a problem with my dog and my vet told me to call you." I could barely make out the words, so softly was she speaking. I could hear her anxiety, fear, and defeat.

"What's wrong?" I grabbed my coffee and settled comfortably on the couch. This was one person I felt needed to tell the entire story without interruption.

"I have a two-year old Border Collie who attacks everyone who comes to my trailer. I think she's aggressive and I want you to look at her. She especially goes after my father and brother and has bitten both of them. I'm getting ready to move and she can't do this in the new place. Will you look at her and tell me if she's aggressive? If you think she is, I'll have her put down."

"Certainly, but could you tell me a little bit more about what's going on?"

Hesitantly she began to recount a tale of alcoholism, abuse, Alzheimer's, and anger. She had been taking care of her elderly father and living in a trailer on his property. He had always been an angry, alcoholic, and abusive man, but now it was turned directly at her and, when she was not at home, the dog received the brunt of his rage. This was compounded by the fact the man was slowly sinking into the private world of the Alzheimer's sufferer.

Her brother had grown to resemble the father he so disliked. At each infrequent visit he passed the dog which was tied-up outside the small trailer. As the dog barked furiously at him, he would strike out with a well-aimed kick, or punch, or hurl an object at the tethered Border collie. The dog only redoubled its efforts to reach the man. Both father and son had become the sworn enemies of this dog, and she became aggressive at the sight of them. But, now her anger had escalated to include most people she met.

"Please come early on Saturday morning. If the dog is not aggressive, as I believe it not to be, you can stay for class and we'll get this fixed."

Her response was an almost inaudible thank you and click of the phone.

Saturday morning was clear and the temperature was perfect for working dogs, warm with a soft breeze that never let you get too hot. The birds were in full song, happy with life. My dogs snoozed away in the early morning sunshine which crept across the floor in their kennels. The sheep, which always seemed to comprehend it was Saturday and put distance between themselves and the class, had moved off down by the river and were contentedly grazing while their lambs slept blissfully nearby. The cats, who by common agreement thought it best to ignore the Saturday goings on, had taken up residence on the front porch and would not move until class was over. I sat on the back porch awaiting the arrival of Melanie and her dog.

In concert all heads on the property were lifted and turned toward the gate at the end of the lane. I knew it was time to get ready for work. Tucking a leash into my back pocket, I ambled out onto the pasture and waited.

I hadn't known a car door could be securely closed in silence. I felt as if I were witnessing the dematerialization of a ghost, so effectively did Melanie seem to fade away to nothing as she turned toward me. The

Border collie on the other hand, a beautiful young dog with an athletic build and superb coat, seemed to increase in size as it immediately went into a defensive demeanor. Her eyes were solidly locked on me, shoulders tensed, lip lifted and a low, menacing growl flowed unceasingly from deep in her chest as the two made their way to where I stood.

With head down and shoulders hunched, Melanie spoke just above a whisper, raw emotion barely contained, "This is Bonnie. She greets everyone like this and sometimes she tries to bite. I don't know what to do..." Her voice cracked and she began to cry without making a sound. Bonnie, on the other hand, became even more defensive and menacing.

"Melanie, relax, right now you're making Bonnie very nervous." I couldn't begin to work with her, or Bonnie, while both were in this terrible emotional state; they needed to calm down, come to the realization that nothing awful would happen, and then we could begin. To achieve that goal I had Melanie move to the porch and sit down.

I began small talk, not a great skill of mine, but very important at this moment. I asked inconsequential questions, where she'd gone to school, how long she'd lived in Montana, where she'd gotten Bonnie. As Melanie, in infinitesimal hitches, became relaxed—and visible—again, Bonnie deflated and resumed the proportions of a normal Border collie. Her lip slowly descended covering her teeth, her shoulders slumped to a more normal height, the rigidity of her muscles disappeared, and her eyes began to wander as she took in her surroundings with curiosity.

Smoothly I took up the dog's leash, "Bonnie and I will be right back, we're taking a short walk." Before Melanie had a chance to react we were heading across the lawn.

Bonnie's world pulsated with hate, uncertainty, fear, aggression and, probably, unremitting stress. It was a wonder she hadn't gone over the edge, yet here was the resiliency of the dog mind, she was beginning to show signs of enjoying our walk. After a time, she and I made our way back to Melanie who sat dumb-struck on the porch.

"She's never gone off with another person like that, and she's never looked so relaxed and happy." Even in her astonishment Melanie looked more at ease, too.

"Bonnie is not aggressive, she's merely reacting to all the stress, hostility, and fear around her in the only way she knows how. Your anxiety is a big trigger. You need to stay calm for her sake. She looks to you for behavior clues." I watched Melanie absorb this information.

"She's not aggressive?" Hope tinged the question. "Not the way you mean, no. I want her in class today."

Once again, Melanie began to make herself small, and her stress was communicated to Bonnie, who immediately shot me a glaring look of anger as she perceived me to be the instigator of the discomfort flowing freely from her owner.

My other clients began arriving, singly or in groups of two or three cars, and pulled up and parked against the edge of the pasture. Dogs unloaded with a wide array of behaviors. Those who had attended longest displayed a calm, controlled demeanor, those just beginning their training, or only having attended a class or two, pulled owners unceremoniously toward the dog kennels, the pasture, the creek, or wildly zigzagged as they attempted to explore everything at once.

Melanie hung back, apart from the group, as Bonnie became more and more visibly stressed and inched her way up to a display of aggression. I quickly took the leash from Melanie's hand, guiding Bonnie to a place in front of the group, and had her sit next to me. Within seconds she was calm again.

As I do with each class, I asked the owners how the previous week had gone for them. Some frustration was voiced and we discussed how to deal with a problem. Relief was heard from many as they ticked off a list of challenges encountered and overcome. I warned those whose dogs were at the off-leash level of work that the sheep were out. They needed to be vigilant to ensure they corrected their dogs' behavior at the thought level, before a wreck occurred, and not to be oblivious to the dog, therefore reacting after the wreck had happened and the dog had reached the "I'm-eating-lamb" fait accompli level. There was nothing better to teach owners to pay attention to their dogs' non-verbal communication than the thought of an impending, gory, massacre of small, innocent lambs that an owner had enjoyed watching gambol.

The majority of the next two hours were spent assisting Melanie to release fear and stress. I felt like a therapist as I listened to terrible memories and narratives of horrors encountered. I quietly, but firmly, repeated to Melanie that she needed to let go in order to help Bonnie become the best dog she could be—that it was her insecurity, stress, and emotional upheavals that were causing Bonnie's problems. I drew her back, again and again, to the fact that she had walked off with me that morning, a completely different dog emotionally. She had dropped all problems and dealt and reacted only with the 'here and now' that was our walk. I wasn't certain I had gotten through, but I sent them home with specific instructions on what I wished them to master in the coming week. The second Saturday of Bonnie's instruction didn't bode well as I assessed Melanie. She was still overly tense, unsure, and self-effacing, creating many of Bonnie's behavioral problems. Again, we did little work on Bonnie and much work on Melanie. This Saturday ended at exactly the same place the previous one had ended. I wondered if Melanie would be capable of changing.

I worried, thought about, and discussed Melanie's situation that entire week. I'm certain my fiancé, Ric, was exasperated by Friday night and wished we hadn't gone out to dinner as the conversation was all Melanie and Bonnie. I wanted the key to Melanie and didn't feel as if I'd found it. I knew it existed, but it wasn't within my grasp and I felt as if I were failing Bonnie somehow.

I had been through a terrible divorce which took almost three years to finalize. I knew what my stress had done to my dogs and their behavior, and I felt well-versed to aide Melanie with her problem. I had been forced to confront the fact that what I was communicating to my dogs, in a non-verbal manner, was my insecurities, anger, frustration, worries and unhappiness, and it affected my dogs deeply, as the leader they depended on conveyed the message that their world was about to implode. They mirrored many of my issues as they lived with growing stress and fear. It was not a good time for any of us, and I wanted to change the same scenario for Bonnie. I just wasn't finding the right words to help Melanie and I was becoming frustrated. Then I found myself frustrated because I was frustrated. The cycle had to come to an end, and it happened the Saturday of the third class.

Seeing Melanie with the same fearful, defeated demeanor sent me over the edge. I had lectured, explained, been understanding, and supportive, but now, it was time for straight talk as I realized that Bonnie, too, was nearing the end. Having experienced moments of calm, even enjoyment, in class, the dog was really suffering from Melanie's constant negative emotional barrage.

"Steve, please take Bonnie on a walk with you and Chloe," I asked of one of the most competent, calm owners, whose own dog, Chloe, was relaxed and well-behaved. I trusted that he would take good care of her, as he could read dogs well and would know how to deal with Bonnie should she turn fearfully aggressive. He smiled and quietly took the leash, leading her back to where Chloe sat waiting.

"She doesn't like men, she'll....." The

fear in Melanie's voice was clear and carrying, and Bonnie turned to look back over her shoulder. Before the dog could react, Steve talked quietly to her and continued on his way. Bonnie fell in beside him without a problem.

"No, Melanie, you're wrong." I struggled, but knew I was failing to keep the frustration out of my voice, because just like dogs, this woman needed a calm, strong leader to point the direction and insist it be followed for the good of all. "Bonnie doesn't have a problem with men—she has a problem with you." Shock registered on Melanie's face and her eyes filled with tears.

"Listen carefully, because you're hurting your dog. Your emotions are driving her to aggression and she IS going to bite someone, and then she'll probably be put down because of her constant aggressive actions to all people. Is that what you want?"

To me, we were now at a crucial point: either this woman understood what was at stake and changed, or she didn't. If she couldn't change, then I would try to get her to release the dog to someone willing to adopt it. If I didn't, Bonnie didn't stand much of a chance for survival.

"Bonnie has two problems. She doesn't like your father and brother, and rightfully so. They have taught her that they'll be cruel to her and she responds in

a defensive manner when she sees them.
This problem is specific to those two people,
and only those two. But, that will change
in a couple of weeks. It will be gone from
her life.

"You, on the other hand, are with
her daily and your fear and unhappiness
are flooding her every second." I was now
lecturing to a bowed head. "She doesn't
know why you're unhappy and afraid, she
just knows that when it's the two of you,
alone, you're not that way, or at least not
as much that way, but when people come
onto the scene you crank up into a fearful
state. What's she supposed presume from
this? People make you fearful, therefore,
people must be the problem. She does the
only thing she can—she tries to protect
you, and herself, from what's making you
afraid. Bonnie doesn't realize that what
you're experiencing comes from your history with your father and you're afraid that
because Bonnie's been aggressive with him,
she's an aggressive dog at heart, and will
be aggressive with all people. Stop it. You
have to get a grip on yourself." My anger
was winding down as I took in the slumped
shoulders, the bowed head, and the tightly
clasped hands.

"She's not aggressive with me," I took
a more reasonable tone. "Look, she's not
aggressive with Steve—and he's a man she
doesn't even know. She's not aggressive

with anyone in class." She raised her head and turned to watch Bonnie playing with Chloe as Steve walked them to the highest point of the property. "You're moving soon, you need to offer Bonnie a new life without fear. That means you can't be fearful as Bonnie looks to you to tell her how to behave and what to expect in each new situation and with new people. How you feel tells Bonnie how she should feel."

"I don't want her to feel afraid, I love her..." the words struggled to come out past the pent-up emotions.

"I know. That's why from this moment on, when you're with Bonnie, you're going to believe in her. You're going to let her know, by being happy and calm, that she's a good dog with nothing to fear." I thought I saw a glimmer of understanding in Melanie's eyes as she continued to watch Bonnie romp with her new friends. "You're moving. You should be happy that you're getting out of that hell-hole, and that happiness is what Bonnie needs from you. Give her your confidence, give her your happiness, and you'll have no problems. I promise. Now, go get Bonnie and you and Steve take a walk together with your dogs. Do NOT think about your father or home, just how happy Bonnie is right NOW."

"Alright," Melanie looked at me, straight in the eye, the first time this had ever happened. She walked off and I hoped

I wasn't imagining that she held herself more confidently.

The next two Saturdays saw huge differences in both Bonnie and Melanie. I could tell that things were improving. Bonnie, by nature a dog willing to be social and well-behaved, blossomed around the other people and dogs and Melanie did the same. Bonnie's enjoyment of class made Melanie happy, and Melanie's happiness increased Bonnie's joy. This was a circle I always loved to see develop.

I offered a sixth, and final, private class for the two of them that introduced Bonnie to sheep. She took to it with the natural avidity of the working Border collie and when finished, was tired, but satisfied.

The three of us headed for the porch where cool drinks waited. As we settled into the chairs I said, "Bonnie is a good dog. I know you don't have stock work for her, but here's Steve's phone number. He does Frisbee competition and he may know of a group near your new place that you and Bonnie can join. You've come a long way, look how happy Bonnie is...you've done a wonderful job."

Melanie sat back and I saw a small smile of satisfaction and pleasure on her face. She was happier within herself, too, I could tell. It would take quite a while for Melanie to gain control over her emotions so that she could offer Bonnie better leadership. But, as of now, she and Bonnie were truly well on their way.

Melanie and Bonnie moved one week after the final session together. It was almost two years later I received a Christmas card with a picture of the two of them. They both looked much happier. The printed line in the card read, "Peace on Earth." Beneath that Melanie had written, "We have both achieved it."

Bonnie, Border collie, age 2

Bonnie had many issues: she was tied-out, she felt defenseless, her owner was an emotional wreck, the majority of all interaction—physical, mental and emotional—was highly charged and negative, she was isolated from her 'group/pack', and wasn't taken on walks.

There is huge confusion within many people as to the difference between an aggressive dog and a dog acting aggressively. The majority of dogs brought to me for aggression issues are not aggressive at all in the true sense. They are frustrated and/or fearful and channel their display of these emotions in an aggressive manner (the currently used term for this is 'displacement'). This is not to say they won't bite, all dogs are equipped with the defensive/offensive biting ability in order to survive, I'm merely stating that just as some humans yell, some slap, some cry, some dogs bite when frustrated or fearful.

What I know, from years of observation, is that dogs that are tied-out, put on the end of chains, attached to run-lines, or staked to posts in the ground, are more apt to be aggressive in their behavior and it's from sheer frustration for many of them, and fear for some of them. In almost every case where a dog is tied, it rarely receives adequate emotional interaction with its humans and is not given supervised exercise, social, and exploratory time.

This is compounded by the fact that the dog feels vulnerable, as the chain inhibits its ability to give ground to an aggressive approach by another dog or human, and it cannot seek a place in which it feels it can sufficiently protect itself. Even humans will search for a safe place from which to defend themselves, such as putting a wall behind them in order to "protect their backs." Dogs on chains are often denied this security and learn early to go on the defensive in order to drive, what they consider, potential threats away. This learned behavior is then exhibited any time they begin to feel uneasy. If the chained dog is primarily at risk from other dogs, then it will go on the offensive with all dogs, regardless of the situation. If the threat is from humans, then humans will be the object of the dog's aggression.

A constantly restrained dog may become overly excited when humans or other animals approach their limited area, as they are starved for mental and emotional interaction. This can also hold true for a dog relegated to a backyard status, though owners are often at a loss to explain why the dog is behaving in such a manner as "he has a nice, big yard to run and play in."

To put this in human terms you can understand: I am locking you in your house; you may not use the phone, answer the door, use the computer, or have anyone over for a visit for one month. How long are you going to last before you begin to go nuts? How are you going to greet the first person you're allowed to see after a month? Calmly and with self-control, or will you, in all probability, make an idiot of yourself, talk too much, get a little pushy, maybe even desperate, when the person indicates it's time for him to depart?

What if someone enters the house, but you are sent to your room and the door is locked behind you? Will you sit quietly on the bed, or scream, pound on the door, demand to be let out? That's what the isolated dog is doing when it barks, jumps, chews, whines and, generally, makes a racket when tied-out. This will also be seen in dogs that are kept in kennels unendingly. They will jump against the kennel doors, bark, and may even show aggressive tendencies out of frustration. Both indicate a dog that is not receiving emotional attention and physical outlet. The tied-out dog has the added fear of vulnerability to attack.

In Bonnie's case, the fear was justified as both the brother and father were physically abusive when dealing with her. She learned early that the approach of these two people did not indicate food, warmth, affection, or positive interaction, but a threat. She responded in an aggressive manner, she went on the defensive.

When Bonnie did have interaction, it was with Melanie, who non-verbally, communicated anxiety, fear, stress, and unhappiness. These emotions increased when in the presence of her brother and father. After Melanie observed Bonnie's aggression to these two individuals, she became worried that Bonnie would behave aggressively with all people. So, the few times she took Bonnie for walks, Melanie's fear and anxiety increased at the approach of each new person. Would Bonnie not like this person and try to bite him?

Dogs, like humans, are all different in temperament and ability to handle pressure. Often people will tell me their dog is fearful, when in reality it is just a dog more sensitive to pressure. They need less emotional pressure placed on them to achieve a

certain reaction—good or bad.
In a simplified example, think of dogs
like radios. Some radios can only pick up
powerful stations, these are dogs that can
take, or need, a lot of pressure for a reaction—their owner needs to broadcast their
emotions "loud and clear" for the dog to
pick up on the fact that the owner is not
pleased, and the dog handles the pressure
just fine. Usually, these dogs are called
stubborn or hard-headed.

Some dogs can pick up moderately
powerful stations. Because they are able to
pick up emotions broadcast at a lower wattage (meaning you don't need be extreme in
your feelings to get a reaction) they respond
more easily to their owner's displeasure.
They tend to be the dog easiest for most
owners to train and handle.

Then there is the dog that can pick
up the weakest of broadcasts. This is the
kind of dog that is so receptive it picks up
an immense amount of emotional communication easily, and may even over-react to
pressure.

Many times this sort of dog is considered fearful when it's actually just overwhelmed by a barrage of emotion from the
owner.

Bonnie was this last type of dog. A
displeased look was all she needed to understand, or think, that Melanie was not
happy with her. The problem with this type

of dog is it doesn't differentiate where the emotion is aimed; it picks up on the emotion and doesn't like it. It takes time for dogs such as these to learn the difference between your being upset and your being upset at THEM.

Melanie was "broadcasting" her personal emotional problems at high wattage and Bonnie was overwhelmed by the emotional equivalent of ear-piercing "static" because she was capable of picking up nuances in emotions. Bonnie couldn't control the volume or change the station and Melanie was unaware of the effect her fears and anxieties were causing Bonnie.

Bonnie could only interpret the world through Melanie's emotions. Melanie was part of Bonnie's "pack" and things would be fine when it was just the two of them. Melanie was relaxed and at ease with Bonnie and they shared affection. However, when they went out, Melanie began to "broadcast" tense, insecure, worried, and upset emotions each time a human approached the pair. Bonnie could only interpret this one way; humans were dangerous and, therefore, must be driven away for the protection of both Bonnie and Melanie.

When I took Bonnie for our first walk I wasn't worried about her aggression, people, a problem, or what might happen. It was simply a walk with a dog. It took Bonnie almost half of our walk to truly relax and start to enjoy it. But, enjoy it she did, as she picked up on my low-key contentment. In the 60s it would have been called "vibes" or "positive waves."

Once Melanie gained emotional control over herself, began to trust and communicate that trust to the dog, Bonnie started to emotionally read the world, and the people in it, as a good place. Bonnie no longer needed to see fear in each new encounter. When she no longer became aggressive when meeting new people, she was able to behave calmly and the people responded with pleasure at meeting her. Bonnie began to experience positive emotions with almost everyone she met, which reinforced her good behavior and taught her to look forward to meeting people. Bonnie no longer needed to behave aggressively because Melanie didn't emotionally cue her to worry about the people she met.

It had all stemmed from Melanie. By changing her, we were able to offer Bonnie the opportunity to change. The more Melanie controlled her emotions around Bonnie, the more the dog calmed down and the more Melanie trusted her to behave. The more Bonnie was trusted, the more she was taken places. The more places she went with Melanie, the less bored, frustrated, fearful, and the better behaved Bonnie became. The better behaved Bonnie became, the more positively she was greeted and embraced by strangers. The more positive interaction with strangers, the more Bonnie became confidently social, until no aggression was seen.

Both Melanie and Bonnie were happy and content, no longer isolated, but spending a great deal of time together, benefiting from a good, loving relationship, free from fear, anxiety, and worry.

Questions & Answers

Q: "My dog, now four-years old, bit a person when he was much younger and he's never bitten anyone since. But whenever we meet someone new, at home, in public, or on a walk, he hunches his shoulders, growls the entire time, and doesn't want to greet them. I warn people he's not really friendly because nothing I do convinces him that it's OK and to relax. Not a command to stop, or my trying to comfort him helps. We took the dog to obedience class, but I'm still afraid he's going to bite again. Why does he behave like this and is there anything we can do?"

A: Imagine an octopus. Each of the tentacles represents a different problem, all of which are connected to one body—you. Let's examine problems first.

Problem one: the fact that the dog bit someone at some point remains in your mind and, because of this, you have a nagging doubt that the dog may not be trustworthy.

Problem two: what you see, in so far as his body language, is an insecure and fearful dog, both emotionally and behaviorally.

Problem three: you respond with obedience commands because of what you think WILL happen, before anything has happened.

Problem four: your repeated attempts to get the dog to relax when it greets people have exactly the opposite effect of what you want.

Problem five: because the dog is not exhibiting what you consider to be a classically identifiable, I-love-people dog response, you read this as a dog which is not friendly, or has problems.

Problem six: because you're nervous and afraid, you tell other people there might be a problem with the dog's behavior and they, in turn, communicate their nervousness to the dog.

All of the problems (be grateful your octopus only has six, not eight), are attached to the body which runs them. YOU are the body. The octopus is now complete and functioning, albeit poorly.

You, as the leader, control all things and send messages which cause the various behavioral responses from the dog. Most owners send unconscious messages all the time. They don't realize that the leash transfers their emotions like a telegraph line, relaying a clear, non-verbal message. They are then shocked by the things their dog does.

As a leader, you must assess your dog as he is now, NOT what he was. People and animals change. People, on the whole, adapt their environment to their needs and wants. Animals are hard-wired to adapt to the situation in which they find themselves.

The average life-span of a dog alone in the wild is about one year. This is primarily due to the fact that he has no hunting companion, no warmth to share, no relationship for psychological and emotional comfort, and no backup when self-defense is needed. The dog is out there by itself, and it's a hard world.

The dog's ability to adapt is of key importance. He must be able to integrate into a new pack as smoothly as possible. To be unable to adapt to new pack rules, members' idiosyncrasies, or new skills and social expectations, will insure that he be driven out and die. Adaptation is built-in to enable the dog to survive. Of course, he will attempt to change some rules in order that they are more in his favor. But, overall, he will adapt to what is established.

We can change the rules in our "packs"

with no problems. It may take a while for a dog to make following a new rule a habit, but he can accept the changes because of his willingness and ability to adapt.

What often takes place, though, is that the human attends obedience class, learns a "few moves," such as saying sit, stay or any other command once in a while, but is totally unaware of the fact that they are constantly communicating something entirely different emotionally. It's this consistent emotional communication that, then, becomes the rules for the dog. I have often said, and I'll repeat it here, obedience does not get behavior, but behavior gets obedience.

In this dog's case, what it is reading is your nervousness, lack of confidence, lack of trust in him, and his behavior, toward the people he meets. Because he is receiving non-verbal communication which tells him that each time he meets new people you are nervous, he interprets this to mean that the people he is meeting may, in some way, pose a danger or threat. You are NOT communicating that you will decide if there is a problem, that you will take care of it and he need only follow your lead. He feels emotionally adrift and must rely on his own wits and instinct to protect himself.

You then make a bad situation worse by using the same voice and mannerisms that tell him he's done something you like.

For instance, at home you say "sit," he does so, and you say, "good dog" and stroke him. He growls at a new person, you say "it's OK", in the same pleasant voice you use to say "good boy", and stroke him in hopes of calming him. What's he supposed to think? He thinks, "I'm doing the right thing by growling because she touches and talks to me in this manner when I've done something that pleases her." You now have a dog that has been taught to growl at strangers. It's just not the behavior you desire.

The other big mistake owners make is jumping to the conclusion that the dog will do something before it has indicated it will do anything at all. This is based on the fact that you've been communicating incorrectly and the dog has repeatedly reacted in ways that can cause problems. You're ready for a problem, you're waiting for it, it happens. You now feel justified in the fact that you KNEW what the dog would do. By thinking this way, you jump in with a correction, such as a snap on the choke chain, BEFORE the dog has exhibited that it's even thinking of the wrong behavior.

The dog is sitting there, not really caring that a new person is coming along. You, however, not wanting another display of bad behavior, skip right over the nervousness you normally feel, and administer a jerk on the choke collar or leash in order to forestall the problem. Here's where it becomcs convoluted. The dog has only one conclusion it can come to, and it won't be that sitting there behaving himself is what you want and a good thing. It's going to be, "I'm in trouble for sitting here, calmly minding my own business, when I should be on the alert and preparing to defend us against that threatening person approaching". He immediately starts to growl. Once again, you've reinforced a bad behavioral response, but it's based ON YOUR EMOTIONS, not the dog and his behavior.

Each time this dog meets a new person he is bombarded by your emotional insecurities and concerns. These feelings aren't present when it's just the two of you, so the only new thing in the picture is the unknown human. It must be the human which is causing you to worry. And, if you, the leader, are worried, he should be really worried. There you have it, a stressed and worried dog that can't figure out just what this new person will do, but it's obvious that he'll do something, because you're tense and on edge, and you tell him, by petting, that his defensive response is correct.

You also reinforce this feeling by telling the new people that the dog is not stable. Each time he comes into contact with a newcomer he experiences their insecurity and fear. He never experiences a person who is calm, relaxed, and likes him. He is in emotional hell. How can he ever relax and enjoy the world. It's full of people, so it must be full of fear for him.

As for the obedience aspect, the dog is being obedient. I'd bet what he wants to do is bite, run, or hide. You've commanded him not to do these and he's not doing them. So, he's being obedient, but he's far from content and at ease. There it is—obedience does not get behavior.

Not all dogs greet people like long, lost friends. But, because humans have been conditioned to expect that, when it is absent we interpret that to mean the dog is not friendly. Not so.

Many dogs need time to assess the situation. They'll hang back and observe the new people, wait and watch. Let them. Some dogs do this because they are a little insecure. Some are just self-contained emotionally.

We had a dog, Annie, a friendly, easy-going dog around kids, adults, and other animals. But, it took Annie about half-an-hour to warm up to new people. She'd sit back and watch the show, and when she was ready she'd go over and greet the person. We often said that she was more feline when it came to greeting people. Cats, as a rule, don't just rush up and greet you. People don't have a problem with this as it is expected behavior from a cat. They have a BIG problem with it when a dog does it, because that's not behavior they expect from a dog.

In order for your dog to relax, you must be relaxed. What you communicate emotionally is the key to how your dog behaves. You must clearly indicate, through your emotions and behavior, that the world is safe and people in it are not a threat. Take a deep breath and let go of the worry.

When new people come to your house, assign a place for your dog to go and lie down. It can be a dog-bed, the corner of the living room, it doesn't matter. It should be where the dog has a clear view of what's going on, but is far enough away to keep pressure low. Tell the visitor to totally ignore the dog. Let the dog remain in place until you're certain it's calm and relaxed. That may take ten minutes, or it may take half-an-hour. When you're certain the dog is fully relaxed you may offer a release command. The majority of the time, the dog will come and greet the newcomer. Tell the guest to maintain a "no interaction" demeanor. Should the dog wish physical contact, it will initiate it. If not, it may just walk away and get a drink. Sooner or later, however, he will come to meet the person and want to be petted.

By doing all of this in your home, you will relax and gain confidence in your dog. You won't be worried about him growling or biting, you won't communicate your insecurities and worries to the visitor, who in turn won't communicate these same feelings to the dog. The dog will pick up on an entirely different emotional atmosphere and respond completely differently than has been the case in the past. When he finally does greet, he will receive positive feedback both from you, and the new person.

If you're out in public, and run across someone, you still need to be calm. It should be easier because of the success rate at home. Have the dog sit next to you when you stop to greet your friend. Explain nicely to him that you'd appreciate it if he'd totally ignore the dog's presence. Tell him the dog's in training, because it's true. This will relieve the pressure on the dog and he'll not growl. Once again, when you're absolutely sure the dog is calm you may let it greet.

You may need to meet up with 50 people before the dog initiates a greeting on his own. Don't push it. What you're doing is building confidence and self-esteem in the dog as it applies to unknown humans. This may take some time. But, because the outsider will be calm, and eventually be able to interact with the dog in a pleasant, what-a-good-dog manner, the dog will receive nothing but positive experiences and begin to associate those feeling with all people.

Your dog may never be the kind that gaily looks forward to meeting and greeting new individuals. He will, however, be re-laxed, well-mannered, and pleasant in his responses. The world will cease to be a ter-rifying and threatening place for him and he will enjoy people. THAT should be the ultimate goal.

Chapter 3

"Where're you walk..."
Alexander Pope

At the request of both clients and veterinarians I was offering, for the first time in eight years, classes in town. This meant I had to drive about thirty miles in one direction, regardless of the weather. And the weather this evening was foul.

I had twenty-nine people enrolled in the class which was to begin this evening, but I wondered, as I tried to concentrate on the road, how many, even though they lived in town, would show up.

Central Montana was in the grips of, what I fondly call, a 'Saskatchewan Scream-

er " Winds over 30 miles per hour were buf-
feting my truck, forcing it to change lanes
of its own volition. Snow was falling from
the sky, as well as being whipped up from
the ground, which made visibility extremely difficult. The truck's heater, which was
a good one, was struggling to offset the -20
degree air seeping into the interior where I
sat muffled, coated, and gloved.

Random images of the frozen bodies
of mountain men and pioneers flitted across
my mind as I passed stranded, and aban-
doned, vehicles by the side of the road.

Whenever I was swapping weather
horror stories with friends who lived in other states, friends who THOUGHT they knew
what bad weather was, they invariably
said, "Well, it's a good thing we live in the
age of cell phones in case of an emergency,
isn't it?" Taking a quick look at mine, I saw
the bars were still non-existent. I mentally
berated the cell phone company, the state
of Montana (the seventh level of cell-hell),
modern technology which failed when most
needed, and my terminally perky friends,
who regaled me with tales of lost hikers
scaling trees in the wilderness in order to
call for help on their cell phones, all the
while punctuating my thoughts with a wide
range of expletives.

I arrived fifteen minutes early and
fought my way from the truck to the doors
of the building in which class would be

held. Entering, I saw several people standing and waiting. All were as mummified in their down coats and winter paraphernalia as I. It was a good sign that this many people were already waiting. It meant these owners were serious about getting help for their dogs if they'd brave the weather to get here.

Finding a facility in town had been difficult. What would fit the bill was limited. I had looked high and low for a large, open space in which to hold class. It needed to be large enough for dogs and owners to actually move about freely, but not so cavernous that I needed a megaphone. There were a few choices and, as was the case in most medium-size towns, the fee charged was vastly out of line with the quality offered.

I had examined such choices as the Beef Barn at the local fair grounds, a dirt-floored cave with no restrooms and all the traits of a sub-zero wind tunnel. I had also checked out a meeting hall which had recently been built. Both were exorbitantly over-priced. I had finally found this room which had no aesthetics, but would work perfectly, was a reasonable price, centrally located, and had heat and restrooms.

The people were milling about, shedding coats, meeting each other, filling out paperwork, and not paying any attention to their dogs' behavior. I could see impend-

ing disaster with at least three of the dogs
and stepped in quickly in order to forestall
a fight.

After the owners finished filling out
the class sheet, they led their dogs out into
the room. I watched, amused, as they repeated a scenario I'd so often seen: pick a
spot, making sure they weren't too close to
another dog, and try to keep their dog under control, so as not to call too much attention to themselves.

It was an interesting group, to say the
least, with a wide range of dogs. In front of
me stood a Newfie the size of a small horse.
She was 168 pounds, full of energy, and
dancing on tip-toe with excitement at the
thought of all the new playmates she was
seeing; her owner was hard-pressed to keep
her in check.

Across the way was a small Bichon,
dropping "F" bombs at every command his
owner gave. Off to the side was a phleg-
matic Bassett that radiated disdain and
boredom with every huge sigh he offered.

From behind me I heard a scrabbling
of nails on the floor, coupled with wheezing,
gasping, and gagging sounds. I turned to
see Patty, a smallish, pretty woman, fighting
to reel in a lean, athletic black Lab, named
Hemmie, which was lunging and pulling
and excitedly nosing everything close to it.
She was having a difficult time filling in the
form as her dog kept jerking her in different

directions.

At the door was a second woman, Michelle, who also had a black Lab. This dog, solidly-built, with a well-muscled body, gave one the impression of a tank. He had his chin tucked firmly against his chest, his entire body was canted forward at a full 45 degree angle, and he was using his full weight at the end of the leash to propel himself forward by inches in his determination to reach the other dogs and people. I noted the owner was using a Haltie and it did little to stop the dog in his heroic effort.

A quiet woman, very self-contained and obviously worried about her dog's behavior, Michelle gave me a somewhat embarrassed look and tried to make her dog, Juno, sit. He ignored her. The two women moved to take up spots as far from each other as possible.

When, finally, everyone was in place I turned to the group, introduced myself, and began explaining what was planned for the evening. Meanwhile, the two black Labs were hanging from the ceiling.

Hemmie repeatedly jumped up on Patty, made mad rushes at the neighboring dog, almost pulling Patty off her feet, let out ear-piercing barks, and gave a good impression of a maypole dancer as he wound himself, and his leash, around her legs. Patty couldn't concentrate for all of Hemmie's activity. I quickly walked over, grabbed the leash and growled out, "AAHT!!" Hemmie froze in place, stared at me for a few seconds, and then sat down of his own accord.

"If he moves again, do what I just did." I handed the leash back to Patty as she stood staring at me with wonder.

"That's amazing. If that's the only thing I learn, I'll be happy." Her voice was tinged with awe as she gazed down at her now quiet Lab. "He NEVER stops moving."

Chaos suddenly erupted on the far side of the room as Juno, having used up all his patience, unexpectedly threw himself to the end of his leash in a valiant attempt to nibble, if not dine, on the Spaniel next to him. Michelle's panicked, "Juno, NO!" cut through the conversation and caused all noise to cease and dogs' heads to snap toward the potential fight. The Haltie was of no use whatsoever as Juno threw his whole being into reaching an Australian shepherd pup which was now cringing and attempting to hide behind its owner's legs.

"So much for the control factor of the Haltie," a nasty voice in my head sneered. Quickly crossing the center of the human circle I unceremoniously snatched Juno's leash from Michelle and issued an "Aahht" in my lowest, meanest, growling voice which caused every dog in the room to freeze in place.

Kip, the twelve-week old Aussie pup, poking his head between John's knees only far enough to let one eye show, looked directly at Juno as if to say, "Oooo...Are you in trouble now!" I made eye contact with him and his head swiftly retreated out of sight. I had to work hard not to laugh.

Juno immediately returned to high gear, pulling, jumping, barking, and now concentrating on the dog to his left. Michelle's face turned a deep red with acute embarrassment as she didn't know what to do. She kept trying to get a hold of Juno, but his expert salsa moves were defeating her efforts.

I got a good grip on his collar, but this contact only increased his out of control antics. Juno, now torn between his desire to meet Kip, and his unbridled ecstasy at having a new person so close to him, went into paroxysms of joy.

"Michelle," I was gasping with the effort to maintain a strong hold on Juno, who was exhibiting all the qualities of a cross between a psychotic Jack-in-the-box and a landed salmon, "Grab his collar."

It took both of us to hold him in place as I unclipped his leash and removed the Haltie from around his muzzle. Quickly looping the leash, I slipped it over his head, gave it a small pop, and let loose with an "Aahhtt!" He gave me a startled look and went still.

I took Juno to the center of the circle and made him sit. "Michelle, why are you using a Haltie? And, please, don't tell me it's for control, because you just had a demonstration that it doesn't work." Juno was in countdown mode as he prepared to launch into the stratosphere once again. I administered a quick verbal correction and continued as he settled down.

"Halties are an industry gimmick. Dump it. The dog has to do his part by exerting some self-control or all you ever do is fight with him. You'll have three choices: ignore his behavior until he's too old to continue doing it; become extremely severe in your corrections by using a choke chain; or get in his head and make him want to work with you. And I can guarantee that the first two choices are not good, for you or your dog."

"These two dogs," I said, pointing to Juno, whose rear end resembled an hydraulic pump as it continuously raised and lowered, and then at Hemmie, who totally ignored Patty's repeated "aahht" and was giving a good imitation of an overly enthusiastic aerobics instructor, "are what I call 'Meth Labs'." The group's laughter helped ease the tension the two Lab owners were experiencing.

"The original Lab, which is what we think of when we think of a Labrador retriever, was acknowledged as a breed in

1903. It's calm, sensible, loves people, and is an easy-going dog. It's the dog you see portrayed on Christmas cards, snoozing in front of the fire. This new Lab was created by today's breeders who seem to have a hard time distinguishing between keenness to work and hyper-activity. They are so different from the original Lab, as a matter of fact, that the AKC is considering have a sub-breed called the American Labrador. They cannot seem to calm down." Both Patty's and Michelle's heads were bobbing in agreement.

"These are the dogs that are flooding the shelters and rescue groups, because owners can't get them under control. They're good dogs; it's simply that we don't have an active enough life-style to offer daily 50 mile treks in order to tire these dogs."

As I spoke these words, the lady with the Bichon gazed down at her dog with a beatific look of gratitude and relief. It was at that exact moment that both Hemmie and Juno made eye contact. Like called to like, and the two nuclear engines, with enough combined energy to split atoms, propelled themselves forward across the cosmic void of class as their owners followed in their wake, like small asteroids caught in their gravitational pull. The Bichon's owner gave a terrified squeak and scooped up her small dog.

"Stop them!" I yelled at the top of my

lungs. Now, I have uttered many stupid things in my life, but I truly believe this one statement takes the cake. It was inevitable. It was pre-ordained. It was Kismet. Like two lovers they ran to each other, oblivious of all else. Their owners, like Montague and Capulet parents, were unable to stop them. In an ecstasy of wild abandon the two dogs crashed into each other, rolled, twisted, leapt, and inextricably entwined their leashes as they reveled in the glory of their connecting. Every dog in class stood and barked their approval as the energy level shot through the roof.

It took some time to regain a measure of calm and separate Hemmie and Juno. Both Michelle and Patty were winded as they dragged their dogs, looking longingly over shoulders to the soul-mate discovered, back to their respective places.

The remainder of class was punctuated by "aahhts" from both women as they tried hard to make their dogs calm down and listen. Hemmie's energy level nosedived first, and he suddenly sat calmly without further correction. It was two solid hours of intense struggle before Juno hit the wall and sat quietly, which was a relief for all concerned.

I watched as the class departed and called Michelle and Patty over. "You both have tough dogs. They need a LOT of exercise."

Michelle's shoulders slumped and she dropped her gaze to the floor. "I can't walk him, he's so out of control."

"It's a nightmare," chimed in Patty, "He pulls, lunges at everything, barks at every dog we pass, I'm exhausted before we even make it around the block."

"I really do know what you're up against. But, you need to understand that both these dogs can't behave calmly because they have no point of reference. If dogs can be out of control on a scale from one-to-ten, these two BEGIN at a five. Five is calm for them, because they've never experienced anything lower. We have to find a way to use up that energy or they can't learn." I was trying my best to encourage both women as I felt they were perilously close to giving up on their dogs.

"I'll call you both tomorrow and set up times to come over and we'll figure out an exercise routine that should do the trick." I let them both go and headed out into the cold.

By late that week the weather had warmed and I'd visited both Patty and Michelle, and even though both were walking their dogs twice a day I was hard pressed to see it. Michelle was having the hardest time as she was single, worked fairly long hours and, while she never stinted Juno on his walks, extra time was hard to come by. What I was going to demand of her took a dedicated owner, and I hoped she had it in her.

On the afternoon that I visited Michelle, I took along a harness and a dog backpack. "There are two types of energy we need to drain from Juno, mental and physical." I was trying to talk to her while the 'Big Boob', as she called him, tried to squeeze between us on the couch. When that failed, he turned quickly to chewing on my shoe laces. I gave him a correction and, without turning a hair, he went for the next weapon in his arsenal, shoving his cold, wet nose in my ear, while offering deep, soggy sighs.

"Quit," I fairly shouted at him. Juno sat abruptly and fixed me with a look intended to create a feeling of guilt. It might have worked if I hadn't seen the underlying plan of action being formulated in his glowing eyes. Within two seconds he was dashing madly between the couch and kitchen and emphasizing his presence each time he neared us by barking loudly, one time.

"Oh, enough of this," I spit out and grabbed him by the collar. "We're going to the river and he can play fetch."

What transpired next was worthy of a full-fledged Sumo wrestling championship. Juno dropped to the floor, rolling, flailing his paws, and licking every part of my exposed skin. Repeatedly, I pushed his head away from my hands, and he exploded with loud, very wet sneezes, spraying my face with a coating I was forced to wipe away in order to be able to see, as I continued struggling to slip the harness over his paddling legs. I would no more get the left leg in, when he'd slip the right leg out of the other side. His rolling, contorting body made its way under the coffee table with me grimly hanging on and slithering in pursuit. His joy at the discovery of this new game was unparalleled, and soon he was attempting to sit in my lap as I vainly tried to buckle the harness. It was a psychotic game of "Twister" with Juno calling colors that were not on MY mat. Getting the harness on him, finally, we went out the door.

The minute he understood we were going for a ride in the car his joy and energy knew no bounds. He barked, twirled in circles, raced from the back door to the garage, bounding unabashedly, and knocking over patio chairs. As Michelle opened the car's rear door, he took a flying leap of about eight feet, sailed neatly across the concrete drive and, never once touching the car's back seat, slammed into the door on the opposite side. Sitting up, he radiated pleasure in his feat of agility. He hadn't felt a thing.

In less than two blocks my respect for Michelle went up several notches. Juno jumped from back to front seat no less than ten times, left streaks of dog slobber in a fair imitation of Arabic script on the rear windows, did his damnedest to fit up on the back window ledge and locked and unlocked the electric doors too many times to count.

"How in God's name did you get him to class?" I gasped while I struggled to keep the seventy-eight pound dog from, once again, sitting on her lap.

"I put one seatbelt around his back hips and the other through his collar" she ground out as she pushed his head away from hers.

"Has he...Juno, stop it!" Having decided that jumping from back to front did not achieve the acceptance he'd hoped, Juno was now slithering over the seat back and onto my lap. "Has he always been this hyper?"

"Yes." Michelle was speeding as fast as she dared through the residential section in an attempt to reach the river before we were all killed.

"How..." I grunted, pushing Juno back another half inch, "...old is he?"

"Eighteen months." She stared resolutely ahead. I would have been frightened by her grim, determined look had I not been preoccupied with Juno's intent to personally demonstrate Newton's second law of physics.

Once at the river I explained what the

first phase of Juno's new exercise program consisted of as I tied a lead rope through the top of the harness. "We're going to throw sticks as far out into the water as we can, then we're going to walk up-river and make him swim to us against the current. That should help use up a great deal of energy."

Michelle began picking up small branches and sticks as Juno towed us toward the water. At the river's edge I dropped the excess coiled line, over fifty feet long, at my feet, while Michelle kept a firm grip on her dog. "Make him sit before you throw it," I cautioned.

After a few minutes, in which Juno never did achieve a sit, Michelle asked, "Should I just throw it?"

"Sure." It was more important to me at this point to lower Juno's energy level than to fight for a sit.

Throwing the stick as far as she could Juno went motionless for a nanosecond then exploded out into the water, the rope snaked out after him.

"Come on, let's walk up this way." We turned and headed away from Juno who now had the stick firmly in his mouth and was paddling toward us.

"Why the rope?"

"Because this river has a strong current and we're going to push Juno until he's really tired. I don't want him to suddenly get to the point where he's too tired to swim back. If that happens" I informed her, "We can pull him in."

For the next hour Michelle and I alternated throwing sticks. "He's tired, look." Juno no longer charged out of the river, splattering us with his enthusiastic shaking. He walked out, dropped the stick, gave a quick shake and flopped to the ground.

"Don't you believe it" I replied. "He's just winded. We'll keep this up another ten minutes."

"Really?"

"Yep." I threw another stick.

Juno lasted another fifteen minutes. On the last stick he hurled himself to the ground and, finally, refused to play fetch any longer.

"I have never seen him do that" Michelle voice registered disbelief.

"Yeah," I said with relief. "Well, now we walk." I began loading the sides of the backpack with rocks and then, calling Juno to his feet, I settled the pack comfortably and securely on his shoulders. "Most of the stupid is out of him, we should be able to get a good walk in. Now, when he's tired, is when we begin training. He doesn't have enough energy left to fight or ignore our commands." I handed the leash to Michelle.

Old habits die hard and Juno, mustering reserves of energy, immediately began to pull, but his efforts were half-heart-ed and within less than a hundred yards he stopped.

"Wow" her tone full of wonder, Michelle smiled and said, "He's actually walking like a real dog!"

The three of us continued on our ramble for another forty-five minutes. "He gets so excited when he sees we're going in the car." Her trepidation came through loud and clear.

"He only has enough energy left for pleasure, not excitement. You'll see." My confident tone seemed to put her at ease. "When we reach the car, he needs to sit, we'll take off the pack and then, when you think he's ready, you can tell him to load up. But, not before you say so."

Juno waited, for the first time in his life, patiently and calmly, until Michelle gave him the command to get in the car. He got up on the seat quietly and sat gazing placidly out the window as we drove home. Upon entering the house, he went to his dog bed, laid down and giving a large sigh, went quickly to sleep.

Before I left I explained to Michelle she'd need to continue this regimen, twice a day, for the next week or so and after that we'd adjust it. As she walked me to the door, she kept looking back over her shoulder in amazement to where Juno still lay dead to the world.

"I haven't been able to get to a door

without him making it a fight for...I don't remember how long." She radiated joy. "I think I'm going to like this."

At Patty's house, the next day, I was greeted by Hemmie who raced to the door, hurled himself upon the woodwork, bounced off and ran back to the back door where he, once again, caromed off the wall and turned to make a dash for the front door. On his fourth pass, Hemmie was adroitly captured by Patty's husband, Jim, who wrestled the dog to an adrenalin-rush, quivering sit. Never releasing his hold on Hemmie, Jim introduced himself and the three of us sat and talked about what to do with the energy leak that Hemmie sprang at every event in his world.

Meeting Hemmie's needs was easier in this house as it had two people to share the load of exercising him. I discovered that the pair had a treadmill in their basement and so we made our way downstairs.

Hemmie exhibited fewer, less intense, and shorter-in-duration energy spikes than had Juno. I explained to the couple how best to juggle morning and evening tread-mill time between the two of them and then left it up to them as to how they wished to handle the subsequent forty-five minute walk.

I had Hemmie walk up onto the tread-mill and stand between my legs while I balanced on the non-moving edges. Slowly I started the belt.

"You need to start very slowly and build up the speed of the belt or the dog will be catapulted off the machine" I warned. Hemmie had no problem being on the treadmill. Hemmie had no problem with the hum of the engine. Hemmie, however, gave me a startled look when the belt began to move. This morphed into dismay as it increased in speed and then changed to disbelief and froze into a look of panic as the ground under his feet began to move at a fairly fast rate.

"It's OK, Hem. Walk" I urged him quietly.

Hemmie shot me an "F" bomb of mega wattage and in an act of gymnastics which would have earned him a spot on the Russian Olympic team, raised straight up in the air and landed with all four feet on the solid edges, two to each side, of the treadmill. He then fixed the moving belt with a look that combined grave distrust with utter disgust and made it perfectly clear that he would have nothing further to do with this enterprise.

The belt continued to move as Hemmie and I engaged in a skit worthy of the Keystone Cops in their finest moment. I would no sooner reposition Hemmie on the machine, than he would manage to get two paws off the belt again and onto the stable edge. In this manner his entire right side was running along with the moving belt while his left paws were firmly anchored on the stationary frame. At one point he managed a tripod arrangement wherein both right paws, as well as his left hind paw were on solid footing and his left front paw ran alone with the machine.

Patty and Jim had collapsed in laughter and couldn't help me. When Jim could no longer stand it, he dashed from the room, returning with the video camera. I am pleased to announce that due to his laughing so hard, the film did not make it to a neighborhood theater.

After a few more adjustments it was discovered that Hemmie did best when a person stood at the front of the machine holding his leash. He was in the zone. No more worry, distrust or escape attempts. He was walking.

The next week's class was better in all senses of the word. The weather cooperated, the people were extremely pleased with the improvements they'd seen in their dogs during the week and both Hemmie and Juno actually walked into class, sat down and were calm.

Patty and Jim were both at class that night and during the discussion period voiced how pleased they were by all the behavioral changes that had taken place in Hemmie.

Michelle was floating three feet off

the ground with pleasure. She had dedicated the entire week to making sure Juno was taken to the river both morning and evening and then walked afterwards for at least forty minutes with the backpack. She simply couldn't contain herself.

"He's so much better. He doesn't charge the door. He can actually sit calmly and wait for his food bowl instead of jumping up on the counter, barking and running through the house. He can ride in the car and stay in the back seat. I took him to the pet store the other day and he sat when I told him to and didn't bother the other dogs that were there." She laughed joyously, "And he lies down now and relaxes. We watched a movie together the other night! But, best of all, I can pet him and he doesn't act like an idiot."

A few people chimed in about how much of a difference they could see in the two dogs in such a short time and both sets of owners were visibly proud. After the discussion period we all went to work.

Halfway through the evening, Hemmie made a bullying move on Hobo, the Bassett. As Patty and Hemmie passed Hobo, Hemmie lunged with a growl and got in the Bassett's face. Patty immediately corrected Hemmie, but her confidence dropped dramatically.

"What's wrong with him? We were doing so well," she questioned.

"Hemmie's just acting tough. You're doing the right thing to correct that. This is not an energy problem, this is an attitude problem," I counseled. "He's a pushy dog and you need to be more intense when you correct him for his bullying so that he understands it's not going to happen in your pack."

A short time later, Hemmie, once again tried to intimidate another dog. He seemed to get a kick out of startling the unsuspecting victim. Patty was at the end of her rope and let him have it with both barrels. Without ever laying a finger on him, she turned her full emotional displeasure on Hemmie. Dogs pulled up in mid-exercise to watch the goings-on.

Hemmie's ear flattened to his skull, he ducked his head and rolled his eyes upwards at Patty, clearly giving her an abashed look which said, "Well, gee, if you feel that strongly about it, I won't do it. Sorry." His behavior changed dramatically and he ignored the other dogs when they passed.

Juno moved to off-leash work that night. Michelle had to be convinced that she could do it, but it was clear to me that Juno had enough self-control now that he could be trusted to listen, self-correct and obey without a leash.

Juno helped Michelle along by not pushing the limits. Now that his energy was at a reasonable level he could contain himself with ease. The more he followed Michelle's commands without a melt-down, the more she relaxed and rewarded him with her pleasure in his behavior. Juno basked in her approbation and she told me before she left for home that night, "I was close to giving him away. I really didn't like him. I couldn't enjoy him because we couldn't just be together, do things together. It was always such a huge effort to do anything for or with him. But, do you know that when we watched the movie he actually sat and put his head on my lap and I petted him without him spazzing out? I've missed having a dog."

Both women finished all the classes with flying colors. Hemmie, the pushier of the two Labs, continued to think up new ways to test Patty. But, in the end, he accepted her as his leader and ceased to test each new rule.

Juno became so well-behaved and trust-worthy that Michelle now takes him to work with her daily and he sits in her office, greeting her clients politely, waiting for their noon walk and evening swim.

At Halloween I received an e-mail picture of Hemmie, complete with devil horns. Earlier that summer Juno had come on a personal visit and was content to sit quietly on the porch as Michelle and I visited.

I felt happy for both dogs and owners, as they'd achieved the goal I set: help-

ing a good dog become the best dog it can
possibly be.

Juno, black Lab, age 18 months and Hemmie, black Lab, age 3 years

Both of these black Labrador retriev-
ers showed the classic symptoms that many
Labs now show: hyper-activity, inability to
concentrate, lack of self-control and an energy level that was beyond most owners'
abilities to deal with.

For these reasons, many Labs are
now almost unadoptable. Often times these
dogs are "failed" in obedience class, as traditional training methods cannot adapt to
their needs. The knowledge of many trainers is strictly mechanical, meaning they
know how to impart an obedience command, but not what is causing the dog's
behavior problem and the best way to deal
with it.

The owners, in the case of both Juno
and Hemmie, were not exercising their
dogs nearly enough, not due to lack of time
or willingness, but because the traditional
walk was not nearly enough to make the
dog manageable for training.

In order for these dogs to succeed
they needed to have their energy, mental
and physical, drained to a point where they
could pay attention, learn and retain what
was being taught. They also needed to be

at a physically manageable level of activity for the owners to be able to interact, and thereby correct or promote a specific behavior.

Simple obedience training was not working with these dogs. It wasn't because they were incapable of learning, but because the training would have needed to either be so forceful as to create a fearful dog or, in the case of positive reinforcement/ treats would only have served to reinforce unwanted behavior due to the association the dog would have made with receiving a treat i.e., I'm feeling very hyper and even though my rear end is on the ground, it's the hyper feeling which is garnering positive attention.

It was important that the owners learn how to drain energy in ways that were productive and didn't continue to allow the dogs to learn or create bad behavior and habits. Once these dogs had experienced the desired level of calm, they had a point of reference for what their owners wanted and could exhibit self-control and return to that point in order to receive positive interaction and affection with, and from, both Patty and Michelle.

Questions & Answers

Q: "We have a three-and-half year old Labrador (black) who is never calm. Since the

day we got him he has been out-of-control
and high-energy. Nothing we do wears him
out. We were told he'd get better around
age two or three, but it hasn't happened.
He takes off and roams the neighborhood,
destroys the garden, chews on the lawn
furniture, jumps on people, can't walk on
a leash and races around the inside of the
house knocking the kids and things over, to
name just a few of his bad qualities. He has
been to three different obedience classes in
three years and nothing worked. We really
love him but we can't take much more of
this and unless you can help, we are seriously thinking of getting rid of him."

A: Have you ever put in a full, physical day
of work and your body is tired, but your
mind is unable to slow down? Because
of your mind still racing, you're unable to
sit and take it easy. This is an example of
draining ONLY physical energy.

On the other hand, have you ever
put in three or four hours of work on the
computer and then HAD to stop because
you couldn't focus any longer and you were
physically tired? This is an example of
draining mental energy.

Of the two, using mental energy has
more effect on the body than just depleting
physical energy. Your dog probably drains
only one-third of his physical energy and
NEVER taps the mental energy. Of course

he'll never settle down.

Many, many, many Labs are now being put on the ground with an energy level which is not compatible with our daily lives. They live in a form of misery which cannot be conceived of by the majority of owners.

Because they never deplete their energy levels they cannot be part of the normal family. They are tied up, kenneled or shoved in the back yard, which makes the problem worse, not better.

The dog, starved for affection, attention from, and inclusion in, his "pack" (the family) reacts with high-energy desperation or excited behavior in his bid for attention. It is not good when any dog exhibits this side of himself, but it is particularly hard to live with when the dog has boundless energy to begin with and his desperation and pushiness can continue almost eternally. The owner, being only able to take so much, begins to pull away from the dog physically, mentally, socially and emotionally. This creates a vicious cycle.

The dog is, literally, overwhelmed by all his choices and cannot physically control himself enough to concentrate on one thing. (We see this with children.) If he cannot concentrate, he rushes from one new experience to another due to a need to release physical energy.

Quantum physics offers us an explanation for some of this uncontrollable behavior.

Within the brain, when a thought process occurs the synapse creates an electrical storm which releases chemicals (peptides) into the body. Every cell in the body has receptors, each with the ability to receive a specific peptide for a certain emotion. Each time the chemical for a thought floods the body, a specific receptor opens to receive the peptides for which they are programmed. Flood the cells repeatedly with the SAME peptide and the various receptors set up to receive a different chemical input will convert to handle the overflow of that ONE chemical.

Flood the cells repeatedly with one specific peptide and the body can't feel normal unless all the cells are fully flooded with the needed peptide.

The out-of-control dog is constantly flooding its cells with the peptide for hyperactivity. Unless the cells are flooded with that peptide, the dog doesn't feel normal and tries harder to create that feeling by behaving in a manner which stimulates the creation of those chemicals which makes him feel normal. It truly is chemical dependency.

Here is the GREAT thing about dogs. Dogs can alter their chemical dependency much more easily than can humans. By changing the thought process of the dog, thereby changing the peptides, the dogs' cells will respond with fewer withdrawal symptoms, in a shorter period of time, than will humans.

By setting up new behavioral patterns the brain creates new peptides and the cells adjust to make the new chemical feeling the normal feeling. It does take time in order to become comfortable with the new feeling, but it does happen and dogs adjust and accept faster than humans.

This is where the owner must decide the type of feeling they want the dog to consider normal. Is it aggression, fear, hyperactivity or calm? I always vote for calm, but it needs to be real calm, not anticipatory calm or calmer-than-I-was.

Really watch your dog sometime when you're making it sit at a door. It will never reach the Zen state of lying on the rug or dog bed, but there are different levels of calm behavior and it is important to insist on the highest level of calm we can achieve.

You ask your dog if it wants out and both of you head for the door. Now, just the word "out" makes the dog excited. HOW excited is the first question. The movement to the door increases the level and amount of adrenalin.

An experienced, well-behaved dog, regardless of age, normally puts out the same level of excitement you or I would at the thought of one of our grown children coming home for the holidays. We are happy and excited, but we're not out of control. This is a moderate and controllable level of adrenalin. He reaches the door, sits in a relaxed mode and waits until you tell him he can go outside. He goes out quickly, but it is not a mad, unthinking dash.

A dog with behavior issues will respond with greater excitement and may run to the door and back to you several times or may run to the door and do jumps, barking and pant quickly and heavily. If you have more than one dog, a small tiff may occur between them. Many people will simply open the door at this point and let the dog out. He pushes past you and races into the yard; he may even pop the door out of your grip in his excitement to go out. You have now set the behavior pattern so that going to the door equals a high to extreme hyper-activity level. He will begin to associate the level of excitement as normal and repeat this behavioral display each time he reaches any door. The more often you allow this excitement level to be displayed, the more normal or entrenched the feeling associated with the behavior becomes. He won't even need you to say "out" to go directly to this behavior in order to behave this way, he'll simply think about going out and then run back and forth to you and the door, jumping and panting when he reaches it. This behavior will even happen when waiting to get out of a car.

Deciding this is not acceptable behavior, you make him sit and wait to be released. Many people equate sitting with a dog's rear end. The dog's rear is on the floor, therefore the dog is sitting. Nope. Watch him carefully. His eyes are glued to the door, his muscles tensed and ready to launch the body, or he quivers with adrenalin and excitement. Just because he's sitting does NOT mean he's calm. You are still encouraging the wrong behavioral association with sitting and/or going out. His mind is racing and far from you. His body is flooded with peptides of excitement. He now associates sitting with high-energy waiting. Not good.

His reactions and feelings will be that from now on when you say sit, he must immediately go on "alert" status. He is not relaxed and this will make staying almost impossible. He will break the sit command at the slightest provocation. Whether that is you saying he may move, opening the door a crack or a cat crossing his path, it won't matter, he was waiting to move, not sitting.

A dog which has learned to associate sitting with being calm will be able to wait with a good degree of self-control. Yes, he wants out. Yes, he anticipates going out. But, he isn't acting like a court jester. He is aware of and focused on you, NOT what waits outside the door. Because he has learned what acceptable calm means, both chemically and physically, he self-induces that feeling and it makes achieving the behavior easy for him. He doesn't feel normal acting like an idiot at the door.

In the case of dogs such as the modern "Meth Lab," which has so much energy that it has NEVER experienced a calm moment, its entire point of reference is hyper-activity. This kind of dog MUST be exercised to a true point of tired in order to experience relaxation. THAT is when you begin training.

If dogs can achieve excitement levels on a scale between one and ten, for example, and the average dog begins to exhibit behavioral issues at a level 3 or 4, then bringing them emotionally back down to a level one or two is not impossible. At any of the four levels these dogs can still be worked with, as the overall range of excitement is still containable. They can think and moderate their own behavior, even if it requires a fair bit of effort on their part. Should this type of dog reach level five or higher, the owner will have his work cut out for him, but still be able to achieve success in behavior modification, and obedience, as the dog has experienced levels one to four.

If, however, "Meth Labs" START at level five, where behavior is becoming out-of-control, how can an owner get control and teach the feelings of level one when the dog has NEVER been calm enough, or drained enough energy, to experience that low level energy and calm behavior? They can't, neither one of them.

Most owners see these high-energy dogs play madly and then stop and take a break. The owner gives a huge sigh of relief, thinking the dog is tiring. He couldn't be more wrong. A break in activity does not mean tired.

Nature has instilled in all animals the need to be efficient. If the energy laid out is not worth the pay-back, then the animal doesn't lay out the energy. For example, a grizzly bear does not walk all the way from Glacier National Park to Great Falls, Montana for a candy bar. The energy produced by eating the candy is NOT equal to, or more than, the energy it took to get it.

Using this example then, a high-energy "Meth Lab" can do or get many things as most of what he engages in is LESS than the amount of energy he has at his disposal. Chewing the siding on the house uses energy, but he still has energy left. So chewing does not leave a negative energy balance and cause a problem. He thinks being calm is a level five energy level as he's never been forced to use up all his energy and function and experience a level one. He has no frame of reference for level one behavior.

Look at it this way. You and your Lab are going to walk across the United States. For the first day or two the Lab has energy galore – level five. He races from you to something new and interesting, back to you, off again to check out the yards you're passing, back to you, down the street, out into the field and back to you. That first evening he is tired and sleeps well. The next morning he's up and ready to go again energy replenished, still at a level five in energy and behavior.

However, after a week of long days his energy level has been drained and each night he is NOT recharging to full power, only maintenance power. He cannot take the chance of running low on energy should what he have remaining be needed for survival, a tough day of walking or self-defense. He begins to forego his mad dashes into unknown fields or yards. He curtails his activities and concentrates on using what energy he has left to keep up with you on the long, daily trek. He doesn't waste energy jumping around when you say sit. He begins to learn, think and consider if what he wants to do is worth the effort considering he may need to use his energy for something more important. When a break in travel comes he uses it to sleep or relax and recharge. He is being efficient with his energy output. He becomes calm because calm takes less energy – he has now reached a level one.

If he remains at level one throughout the entire trip, it will become his normal behavior, even when he has periods of inactivity. Why? Because the feeling of that level has become a normal behavioral pattern for him and is efficient use of his energy.

He is now a calm and thinking dog that can master skills, moderate its own behavior and is easier to handle.

Chapter  4

I Love You to Death

It was surreal. I was watching a small scene lifted directly from the pages of a James Herriot book. This was "Tricki Woo goes Crackerdog" incarnate. A living, breathing (at least I hoped to God the dog was still breathing) tableau, complete with a small, obese, inert form named Punkin laid out on my deck, and three women frozen in a state of shock.

Then, in the blink of an eye, Punkin gave a full-body shiver, lifted her head and stood up a tad unsteadily. Within seconds she was back to her old self, barking, jumping, and rapidly approaching hyper-space behavior, while she rushed madly between us as if she'd never been out cold.

My friend, Ann, raised her eyes to me with a stunned look. Janice's eyes were filled with tears and she was shaking with fright, having witnessed her dog suffer an unexpected seizure. I was very concerned. Punkin continued her ear-shattering yipping while jumping against my leg and then rocketed to the end of the leash to the next person in her insane bid for attention.

I am a devotee of James Herriot books. I devoured them in my early teens. I read the chapter about Tricki Woo with great amusement; I felt, however, that Herriot had used literary license and embellished the recounting for the reader's amusement. Yet, here in front of me was a dog exhibiting the exact same behavior and "crackerdog" symptoms as in the story. It was too surreal. It was worrying. It was a dog that was going to die if I didn't do something.

"Let's get her inside so she doesn't overheat." It was all I could think to say at that moment. I was very concerned that Punkin might have another seizure – one from which she might not recover.

I had watched the green pick-up truck drive up to the house. I had quieted my dogs as they barked in unison with the boarders, and waved at Ann as she came around the end of the truck. Then I looked on in amazement at the clown-and-circus routine unfolding before me as Janice tried to unload her dog from the vehicle.

Launching herself across the front seat, and almost clearing the hurdle of Janice's shoulder, sailed Punkin. Wriggling, barking frantically in a pitch that would shatter glass, panting as if she'd reached the peak of Everest sans oxygen support, and with the agility of a big-top acrobat, Punkin dragged herself over Janice's shoulder and half slid, half ran down her owner's back, hit the ground heavily and sped to the end of her leash, where she flipped herself over backwards and managed to land upright on her feet. Twirling in a circle, hitting high notes which a coloratura would envy, and panting like an obscene phone caller in between the displays, the dog never stopped moving or shut up. I was having a difficult time discerning the breed, but I knew it to be a smallish dog with a lot of hair.

Ann and Janice performed a strange dance only fit for the French court as they made their way toward me and attempted to avoid the nipping, barking embodiment of a Fury on the ground between them.

Ann and I had first met some years ago when she brought her own dog, Mandy, to me as a puppy for obedience training. We had a great time together while we worked Mandy on those Saturday mornings and we had formed a close friendship. Ann was also Janice's friend.

For several months Ann had been calling in great concern saying she was trying to convince Janice to bring her dog to me for help, recounting Punkin's numerous problems. The dog was grossly obese, bit people, was unaware of social niceties, was coddled, spoiled in many areas, ignored in many others, and even Ann could see it was obviously unhappy.

Punkin couldn't interact with other animals as she was incapable of settling down. Other dogs tended to attack her and she was rarely walked for she lunged at every living thing that came into view. She attacked Janice's cats at every opportunity, used the house as a bathroom, tore up the sofa and chairs in the living room, ate the television remote, clawed the entry door to shreds and decimated throw rugs. One would have thought she'd stay svelte with all the energy she was using in her attempt to demolish the world around her. But Janice and her husband fed Punkin snacks, human food and treats, as well as a full bowl of dog food twice daily – and Punkin ate it all without hesitation or guilt. Top all of that off with Punkin's constant movement, excessive panting and barking, and her owners were at their wits' end.

I discovered she was a small Pekinese mix, with a honey-and-cream colored coat, short legs and a tilted way of holding her head while looking at a person that was engaging. She should have weighed about ten pounds; instead she weighed twenty-six. Her visage brought to mind a cartoon character which had inhaled an excessive amount of helium until the body was an over-large balloon with four little protuberances for legs. She didn't walk - she rolled with the gait of a drunken sailor. Her eyes bulged, were slightly glazed and held a desperate look in their depths. Here was a dog screaming its confusion as to why it was disliked by others; screaming in its agony of carrying so much excess weight; screaming from loneliness; and, most of all, screaming to be saved from its owners' love. I wondered if Herriot had felt as awful as I did at that moment.

"Tell me, Janice," I paused in mid-sentence and corrected Punkin in an attempt to make her return to a sit and calm down, "What's going on with her?" I uttered the correction sound again as Janice began to explain about her dog.

"Punkin is four years old and she's bitten a few people, mainly family members because no one else will visit us any more. She causes fights with other dogs, terrorizes the cats, cannot control herself around people, never sits still, never relaxes, is never quiet, and is now biting the mailman, or trying to, and I'm afraid that she'll be taken away from me because of her behavior."

I half-listened as I insisted, again,

that Punkin return to a sit. I had already lost count of the number of times I'd issued a correction for breaking a sit. Punkin was in serious distress and I felt it imperative she calm down before she had a heart attack – literally.

"I love her, but no one else does."

"Uh-huh," I concentrated hard on conveying my insistence to Punkin that she stay seated.

Janice was now reciting excuses for her dog's behavior, "I work long hours and am away from her most of the day. My husband won't make her do anything. He says she's my dog." Her voice was tinged with ire, "He feeds her anything to make her leave him alone. I can't control what he does, especially if I'm not home when it happens. I know he doesn't like her behavior, but he's not helping. Soon my sister and her kids will be coming to visit for the summer and she's told me that if Punkin bites one of the kids, I'm responsible. I love her more than anything, but she doesn't listen and won't behave." She bent down as she said this last part and made a move to pet Punkin.

"Don't." My command was sharp and harsh. I had just managed to get the dog to slow down one notch and Janice's movement had sent Punkin even more out of control than when she'd first arrived. I heaved a huge sigh, "Don't touch her, please. She has some serious problems and right now your touch will not be helpful." Janice looked hurt and embarrassed as she tucked her hand under her arm.

For the millionth time in fifteen minutes I corrected Punkin to make her sit. Her rear hit the ground and bounced back up. I decided to become serious in my correction and sternly growled "aahht!" Punkin's body froze for a nano-second, her panting still at a rate that would induce hyperventilation if I didn't get it under control quickly and then sat, all on her own. Her sitting, however, didn't lessen her barking. Her head continuously swiveled to take in Ann, Janice, myself and her new surroundings. She quivered, shook and managed to scoot around while keeping her rear end plastered to the ground. It wasn't calm or pretty, but it was a beginning.

"Janice, this dog is going to die if you don't get this under control." I cut to the chase with no pleasantries. "She's obese. Five pounds on a dog is the equivalent to fifty pounds on a human. Punkin is carrying about 160 pounds of fat. It puts a strain on her heart, eyes, joints, and organs." I shot a look at Janice, who was sitting on the stairs next to Ann. Both women wore a shocked look at this information.

"Add to that the fact she's pushing herself to the brink of destruction with her adrenalin rushes and her hyper-ventilation and you have a heart attack waiting to happen. And that little seizure we witnessed outside? It's a major warning sign. You have to slim this dog down. I see a lot of overweight dogs and they all have behavior problems. I think it's because they all feel lousy carrying all the fat and acting out is the only means they have to communicate how lousy they feel." I was serious and I only hoped I could convey the enormity of the danger to Janice.

Janice opened her mouth to speak, but I butted in quickly, "And don't tell me how much you love her. Your love is killing her. If you really love her, then you need to do what's best for her, not what makes you feel good."

I launched into a lecture about dogs, their behaviors, their needs and the responsibilities of their owners. Janice simply sat there letting tears track down her face. Ann patted her shoulder and tried to comfort her. The only success I was experiencing was Punkin, who was now maintaining a highly stressed and vocal sit; Janice had obviously shut me out. It was too uncomfortable for her to hear what I was saying, so she ignored me.

"But, you don't understand. Punkin really likes her treats. I give them to her because she loves them and she knows I love her." Janice sniffled and wiped her eyes, "She loves to play fetch. That's exercise, isn't it?"

"No, I think you give Punkin treats because you feel guilty and don't want to face it. You know she's not happy, but giving her treats makes you feel better. Has your vet told you she needs to lose weight?" I countered.

"Yes, and we put her on a reduced calorie dog food." Her tone was defensive.

"Great," I replied at bit sarcastically. "She's on a diet and you destroy it by feeding her everything under the sun in between times. Do you walk her?"

"I used to." Janice looked away, "Ann comes over a few times a week and walks her during her lunch hour."

"Ann, how does Punkin handle the walks?"

With a slightly embarrassed look Ann replied, "She loves the walks and she's a little difficult when we start out, but she can't go far before she's exhausted. We usually make it around the block, but it's hard on her."

"Janice, listen to me, because I'm not kidding, this dog is going to have a heart attack from so much extra weight and her excitement. It has to stop. If you really love her, then love her in a way that's good for her, not good for you." I watched Janice as she once again ignored me and what I was saying.

At that moment, Swirl, one of my most

loving cats, entered the room, eyed Punkin and made straight for us. Janice stiffened in fear and gasped, "Punkin attacks cats."

Punkin caught sight of Swirl and immediately broke her sit and began to pull on the leash, dance around, yip, whine, bark excitedly, and jump on me again.

"I have a mental behavior scale by which I assess each dog when we first greet. It runs from a one, which is the calmest and best, to a ten, which is a dog with no self-control mentally, physically or emotionally." I interrupted myself to try to make the dog calm down. "Punkin, from the minute of her arrival, has exhibited a level ten. I managed to get her down to an eight, but now that Swirl's here, she at about a fourteen." I had grabbed the small dog and pulled her back to a sit position. The second my hand left her back she was standing and barking again and had only one desire; her goal was to catch Swirl. The room was filled with Punkin's hoarse, rapid panting, which was loud in the lulls between her frantic barking lunges.

"This is how she is when the family visits," said Janice with worry.

"What do you do with her when she's like this?"

"It takes a while to catch her, but once we do, we put her in the bedroom." Janice dropped her eyes to the floor. "I've tried holding her, but she bites me and fights to get free."

"Does she calm down when you put her in the bedroom?" I kept a close watch on Janice to see her reaction. Without a word I bent down and put a stop to the tug-of-war Punkin was waging at the end of the leash and placed her back in a sit.

"No. She gets worse."

Swirl, a black-and-white long-haired barn cat that believed she was the Mother Teresa for dogs, calmly approached, her eyes filled with compassion and love. Punkin levitated off the floor, twirled twice, snapped at my ankle and catapulted herself toward her self-proclaimed savior. Swirl didn't bat an eye.

Snapping my fingers I commanded, "Swirl, get back." With the grievously injured look of a missionary denied the opportunity to save the native population, Swirl halted in mid-stride and then quietly turned and went to sit by Ann where she was showered with affection. At least someone appreciates me, her look seemed to say.

"Even the cats listen to you," Ann's voice was full of amazement. "Mine ignore me."

"Cats can be taught, but people don't do it because they're afraid of the claws." I was once again repeatedly insisting that Punkin sit. "I have ten cats, all of them raised around the dogs and the dogs that come to class. They're taught, and expected to follow, the same rules as the dogs. Cats can learn; it's just that people believe they can't."

I had been working for over an hour now to get Punkin to calm down. I was seriously concerned for her health. I didn't think her heart could take much more. I wasn't allowing her to move, but her breathing hadn't slowed, she was still exhibiting high excitement, and teetering on the edge of physical over-exertion.

"There's a big difference between a dog that's healthy and a dog that's fit. Punkin may be lucky and still be a healthy dog, even with all this extra weight, but she's not fit." I explained calmly. "Janice, why don't you take her outside, let her go to the bathroom and then we'll go at it again."

After Punkin and Janice were out of hearing I turned to Ann, "She's killing that dog, you know that don't you?"

"I know. I've been trying for several months to get her here, but she always has excuses." Ann watched the pair through a window as she spoke. "Punkin's a good dog, but they don't do anything with her."

Standing by Ann at the window I watched Janice as she and Punkin made their way back to the house. Punkin zoomed around at Janice's feet like a tethered, psychotic bumble bee, her barking, panting and racing all reflecting her frantic feelings.

Janice did nothing to control or direct the dog's behavior. "I can help Punkin, but if Janice won't see what she's doing to that dog and change, it won't do Punkin a bit of good."

I spent the next forty-five minutes regaining the ground lost when Janice took Punkin outside. Then, suddenly, as if a switch had been thrown, Punkin calmed down.

Janice was astounded and sat with her mouth open.

"Don't get too hopeful," I warned. "Punkin's just run out of steam. But now we can begin to train."

I simply stood and talked about dogs with Janice and Ann while I let Punkin experience a total calm. Her breathing was still a rapid pant, but nothing like it had been. She no longer broke a sit and the look in her eyes was much calmer and outward in appearance. She had lost that glazing of "inward" concentration I often associated with dogs in pain, illness, unhappiness or near death. She was now concentrating on me with a look which told me that she was actually seeing me, not merely skimming the surface of the world around her.

It was time to help Punkin learn to interact correctly with other animals. It couldn't be fun living in an isolated world. I knew Ann couldn't let Mandy visit with Punkin as a fight always erupted. I didn't

believe that it was because Punkin was ag
gressive, but because she felt ill and was
frantic for emotional contact from any
source.

"Newt?" I called out and gave a short
whistle. A black-and-white head appeared
around the corner of the door and popped
between the seated women's shoulders.
"Come here, Bud."

Making room for him to pass between
them, Newt quietly and calmly entered the
room as Punkin caught sight of him and
zoomed back into an overly-excited state.
"Lay down there, old man." Newt lay down
at Ann's feet and quickly eyed both Janice
and Ann, then turned his attention, once
more, in my direction. He watched Punkin with a curious gaze, as if watching an
alien life-form. Swirl began to make purring passes under his chin and bumped her
head against Newt's cheek. He ignored her,
his concentration solidly upon Punkin and
me.

Janice paled and her interlaced fingers turned white with the pressure of her
grip.

"What's wrong, Janice?" I was somewhat astounded at the abrupt and drastic
change in her. I quietly corrected Punkin
into a sit and watched Janice's worry-filled
eyes flit from Newt to Punkin and back
again. I thought she'd calmed down, but
just like her dog, it took very little to unbal-

ance her emotionally.

"Punkin doesn't get along with other dogs." Her concern was so apparent that Newt turned and looked at her.

"Newt's an awesome dog," Ann volunteered. "You should see him work Susan's big rams, or cattle. He's really great, I love him." She reached down and stroked Newt's back.

"Janice," I kept my eyes on Punkin in order to gauge how she was doing, "Newt and I have worked together for a long time. He's retired from stock work now, but he's a steady, calm dog and he doesn't react to pressure. I need him here to help Punkin learn how to behave around other dogs." I broke off just long enough to correct Punkin and watch her sit. We were improving, as I hadn't even had to touch her, just make the correction sound. This meant Punkin was in the moment, was aware and concentrating on her part in the training. It was a huge step forward for her and I was pleased. "You need to be calm and stop worrying. Your emotions are what Punkin is reading and it will make it that much harder for her to do this right if you're nervous, worried or upset."

Janice went silent, but I could see that she wasn't relaxed. I glanced down at Punkin again and saw that she was totally oblivious to Janice and her feelings. I mentally raised my eyebrows. This was a dog that was part of a family, but wasn't Punkin had no real attachment to Janice and that told me a lot. Punkin lived with these people, was given food, shelter, toys and the people believed they showered her with love. But, the reality was the dog didn't consider them as part of her pack. She had wandered through her last four years as a loner, without all the necessary leadership, support and comfort a true pack would have supplied. No wonder she was in the state she was in. I explained all this to Janice.

"But, I love her," she cried desperately.

"That may be, but love in the dog's world is not what makes it secure and healthy, mentally or physically. If love was all it took, we wouldn't need animal shelters or trainers."

"We take good care of her," she broke in, anger tingeing her voice.

"Janice," I explained calmly, "The way you love her is the way you want to be loved. It's not the way Punkin needs love in order to be secure and calm." I stopped briefly as I corrected the small, panting dog from whining. "You think that letting her sit on your lap, giving her treats, petting her each time she comes to you will show her how much you care. But, look at her, she's not happy.

"She can't be with other dogs, she's hated by people she meets because she's poorly behaved, and she's never relaxed around you. Is that taking good care of her? Would you like to live your entire life that way?"

I knew I sounded like I was being hard on Janice, but if there was any hope for a better life for Punkin it would be because Janice saw the truth and changed in order to make that possible.

"Jan, look at her," Ann chimed in. "She's so much calmer now. She actually looks happy being told what to do."

We were now two hours into this session and I wanted to offer Punkin a chance she had been denied for many years – that of making positive contact with another animal.

"Newt, closer..." I called quietly. He responded immediately and rising took three steps forward. "There" I told him and he sank to the floor, watching me and waiting patiently for the next command.

Working with Newt, whether on stock or in the rehabilitation of dogs, had always been effortless. He and I just seemed to mesh without sharp edges. He understood, without my directing him, what was needed, particularly in this instance. He didn't react to Punkin's outbursts, which subsequently grew more infrequent and less emotional. Newt helped Punkin reach a place of calm faster than I might have been able to alone. I had complete and utter faith in him, his reactions and his abilities. We had an amazing relationship; this was what I always attempted to teach my clients to achieve with their own dogs.

Over the next fifteen or twenty minutes I gradually brought Newt closer to Punkin. Each time Newt moved it was necessary to calm Punkin down again. But, these corrections were achieved more quickly each time by the small dog. Her panting was still audible, but nothing like when she had arrived. She held a sit and was no longer whining or wiggling.

"Down here, boy." My final command placed Newt on the floor right next to Punkin, their bodies touching. Newt greeted the tiny dog with a couple of introductory sniffs and then turned his head to follow the path of Swirl who had decided that three's company, not a crowd. The cat snaked her way under Newt's chin, then touching noses with the startled Punkin, slipped around to curl up as closely as possible to the small dog's stomach. Her contentment was evident in her "Evinrude motor" purring. She blinked her eyes twice in the patent cat manner and proceeded to lick Punkin's ear.

From the corner of my eye I caught Punkin looking up at me. I looked down at her and was snared in a set of eyes that were focused and happy. A great contentment radiated from her and I could actually see her relax between the two calm animals. Bliss flowed from her as she succumbed to Swirl's ministrations and snuggled into Newt's side. My dog turned his head, nudged the small form and, turning his head back, placed his muzzle on his legs, closed his eyes and went to sleep. Punkin let out a large, long sigh, closed her eyes and basked in the contact she had long needed. I knelt and slowly stroked the little dog's head. She gave a grunt of pleasure, but didn't move.

Both Janice and Ann sat on the bottom step of the stairs and wept openly. "I never thought I'd see this," Janice whispered. "She's so happy."

"You must help her lose weight, take charge of her behavior, and do what's right for Punkin," I insisted. I hoped with the picture at my feet fresh in her mind, Janice would see that changing how she behaved toward Punkin would lead the tiny dog into a new world and a life full of happiness and health.

"I will," was her fervent reply.

I let Punkin enjoy her moment for a while as we three women sat and talked about nothing in particular. I felt badly about breaking up the small group, but Janice needed to get home. As she walked her small dog to the truck, Punkin repeatedly looked back over her shoulder at Newt, Swirl and me. I saw a yearning in her eyes

and hoped Janice would do as I'd instructed in order to truly help Punkin recapture
the moment of calm, happiness and contentment she'd just experienced.

A couple of weeks later I called Janice to see how things were going, but only
got an answering machine. I then called
Ann and we talked for quite a while. Janice had followed what I taught her for all of
two days and then slipped back to her old
ways. Punkin was, once again, paying the
price. Ann was doing all she could to help
and had taken her lunch hours to go over
and walk Punkin several times.

"She loves our walks, but it's taking
longer and longer to get her to calm down."
Ann's tone mirrored her concern. "She's
back to nipping and running in circles,
panting heavily and the last time I went to
the house she attacked the cat. I don't have
enough time at lunch to wait her out until
she becomes totally calm. I don't think I
can keep going over if it means seeing how
miserable she's becoming."

"Sometimes, the best we can do will
not be enough," I said heavily, "If the owner
isn't willing to see that what they are doing
– or not doing – is the cause of the problem
there's nothing we can do."

We talked about the possibility of
getting Janice to release Punkin, but we
both knew it would never happen. Janice wanted Punkin for her own emotional

reasons, but they were reasons that didn't, and would never, include Punkin's needs. Janice would continue to deny that her love was killing her dog, right up to, and including the moment the small, tortured soul finally quit its struggle.

I hung up the phone. My misery was complete. I wondered if I had been wrong to help Punkin, to offer her a brief moment of respite in her world of hell. To show her how wonderful life could be and what she was missing. I recalled the vision of her total contentment and happiness as she sat between Newt and Swirl. To succeed in helping a dog, while failing to change the owner, guaranteed misery in the name of love. It was the part of my work that always made me feel angry at the human, saddened by the situation and heartbroken for the dog. I began to cry for Punkin.

Punkin, Pekingese mix, age 4+ years

Punkin suffered in many areas, but all her problems had one root cause – her owner. Janice loved her dog.

The majority of owners love their dogs. Some are better at expressing it than others. In Punkin's case, Janice loved the dog for what she got from it, not for a mutual relationship that the two of them shared.

Janice got great satisfaction out of babying Punkin. As a small puppy, Janice carried Punkin almost everywhere. The dog became a substitute for children she'd never had and didn't seem likely to have in the future. Her marriage was shaky and children were not in the picture. She and her husband were distant with each other, even considering a separation. Punkin was showered with physical affection which filled a need in Janice. However, Janice gave no thought as to what Punkin might need from her.

If Janice was blue, or lonely, or needed an emotional boost, Punkin was there to provide it. Janice was so self-involved she couldn't see that Punkin's needs fell by the wayside in her pursuit of self-gratification.

When Janice was forced to acknowledge Punkin's deteriorating behavior, she handled her guilt by offering the dog treats. We often see this in parents who are self-absorbed in their careers or personal pursuits. When their children act out for attention, these parents often respond by buying the child something. The parents mitigate their guilt by substituting an item for an emotion and/or personal attention. Janice was doing the exact same thing, merely using food as the substitute.

This led to Punkin's weight problem. In the wild, dogs do not get fat. Nature has not equipped the dog to deal with the problems associated with obesity. The domestic dog that is obese has no freedom to alter his lifestyle. He usually lives a contained, non-active life – an anathema to dogs – and the excess weight results in his feeling poorly. This constant state of low-level irritation creates behavioral problems and, I believe, the dogs have only one avenue in which to express how sick they feel; neurotic behavior. I often see overweight dogs act out aggressively or hyper-actively. This was the case with Punkin.

Because Janice would not take up the mantle of leader, insist on and teach good behavior so that Punkin could interact socially, and exercise her so that she felt better and could control her energy and responses, Punkin was not included in social outings and family gatherings. Therefore, she was not offered an acceptable means to satisfy her emotional and physical needs.

Punkin used every ounce of energy she had to destroy things around her in order to lose weight. It might have worked had not Janice been using food to assuage her personal guilt.

Punkin also did not feel a part of a pack. Janice had left Punkin to drift and make decisions on her own, but they were not acceptable by human standards. Janice did not provide the bridge between dog behavior and human expectations. Punkin did the best she could, but she only had the skills to be a dog.

Janice's belief that if she loved Pun-

kin enough everything would be alright
only caused insecurity in Punkin, as her
inappropriate behavior with humans and
animals resulted in constant negative responses and she didn't know why.

I believe, and I have seen it many
times, that Janice's overwhelming need for
affection kept her from correcting Punkin's
behavior for fear that her dog wouldn't love
her. Janice was unwilling to change her
behavior, or see what she was doing, if it
meant she might not get her emotional fix.
Punkin, and her emotional and physical
needs, was sacrificed to Janice's expectations and desires. Janice knew something
was terribly wrong in Punkin's life, but if
facing her demons meant Janice had to
deal with her personal problems and solve
them, she wouldn't do that. It was easier
for Janice to ignore what she was doing to
Punkin and let the dog carry the misery,
than fix herself and offer Punkin a chance
at a full and wonderful life – all in the name
of love.

Questions & Answers

Q: "My Cavalier King Charles has gotten
very short tempered. She snaps at our
other dogs, growls when we make her move
and just has a bad attitude. She's about 5
years old, spayed and has become less active. My vet says she's healthy, but needs to

go on a diet because she's about 20 pounds overweight. She doesn't get table food, but we do give her treats and she's always loved them, but now she doesn't seem interested in them. She's always been a happy dog, so what do you think is making her act this way and how do we fix this problem?" Jane R., CT

A: She's obese, feels rotten and you're slowly killing her. A Cavalier should weigh about 15 pounds. I have found that most vets are very careful about how they phrase their warnings where overweight and obese pets are concerned as the owners can get huffy and pull their business. I don't care! Read this next sentence carefully. Every five (5) pounds of excess weight on a dog is equivalent to 50 pounds on a human - your dog is carrying about 200 pounds of fat.

Dogs do NOT need to eat every day. It has been shown that a healthy dog can go five days without eating before there is a noticeable body change. Now, I am not suggesting you starve her for five days, but she certainly needs to have her eating habits changed.

The pet food industry is in the business to make money. With that in mind, they show commercials in which dogs gobble up, with joy and enthusiasm, everything placed in their bowl. They offer empty-calorie treats (so your guilt is abated) and are now offering a wide variety of 'reduced calorie' foods to make more money combating the fat their original foods put on your pet.

Dogs, if left to their own devices, would not be overweight. They would be active, miss meals, and actually stay on the lean side. Mother Nature does not condone obesity; it's the antithesis to a natural lifestyle.

A healthy dog should be within 2% of its ideal weight the majority of the time. You should be able to discern a hint of the rib cage under the skin, and be able to feel the ribs without digging through a layer of fat. Now, don't go envisioning the slum dogs of Calcutta or dogs scavenging through the Mexico City dump. That would be skeletal and a complete opposite to this problem. Either extreme is not good for the dog.

Every dog is born with a certain metabolism, just like humans. Their caloric needs will change with age. Pups, working dogs, pregnant bitches, dogs living outside year round have higher caloric needs. As the dog ages, stops working or activity levels decrease, its metabolism slows and calories need to be reduced. Spaying/neutering does NOT cause a dog to become fat. INACTIVITY and unneeded calories are the culprits.

Dogs are the master of the "I'm starving" look. Don't buy it. It's simply Mother Nature, again, prodding the dog to eat while there's food in order to offset the lean times. The problem is our dogs don't face any lean times.

Free feeding, eating another's food as well one's own, lack of walks, or feeding according to the bag's instructions are usually the primary cause of obesity in dogs. Free feeding results in a temporary increase in bone density which, in turn, causes a false positive weight reading. In the wild, this density would stand the dog in good stead at the beginning of lean times. Density would decrease to genetic normalcy as food sources became scare, but the core bone density would not be affected for a long time, thus, literally, giving the dog a leg to stand on.

Eating another dog's food, as well as one's own...need I say more?

Feeding according to the bag's instructions is not to be taken as gospel. It is merely a guideline. Your dog's food should be adjusted based on its visible weight. Getting heavy? Cut back. Working hard or engaging in long, fast daily walks? You may want to increase the amount.

The reason most vets tell you to feed twice daily is due to the possibility of bloat or choking when your dog inhales its food. It's not because the dog can't manage to last a full 24 hours without starving. Many dogs gobble food even when fed twice a day. Spend some time teaching the dog to slow down while it eats. Lay a hand on its back to break the concentration it's focusing on its food.

Obesity in dogs causes the following: diabetes, joint problems, kidney problems, heart strain, gastrointestinal problems, shorter life span by an average of two years, heat intolerance, and skin problems, to name only a few.

As for your dog, of course she's ill-tempered; she feels rotten carrying all that excess weight around. Psychologically, she can't be happy when she can't play or keep up with the other dogs. Physically she's probably short of breath; everything is a massive undertaking for her and she's constantly tired, hence the decreased activity level and general crabbiness.

Ironically, the stress and strain of the extra weight can manifest in the form of hyperactivity bursts. People incorrectly interpret this display as happiness on the part of the dog. It might also take an aggressive form in which the overweight dog lunges, barks, attempts to fight with another dog, and shows a decided lack of tolerance in areas that, previously, were not an issue, such as determined possession of a specific toy. If the dog experiences enough continuous hyper-active or aggressive displays, and depending on the individual dog this could be for as little as 10-15 minutes, the dog might very possibly experience a seizure, involuntary urination, disorientation or all of them combined, and in extreme cases, a stroke or heart attack because of the excess weight.

Cut back on her food. If she needs to feel full, add a portion of canned pumpkin to her food. Most dogs relish pumpkin with its vitamins and roughage. Make sure it's plain pumpkin, though, not the kind with spices and ready to be turned into pie. The average ratio is one-third pumpkin to two-thirds dry dog food. If, for example, you've been feeding her two cups daily of dry, cut it back to two-thirds cup and add the one-third cup pumpkin.

Get her out of the house and take two or three short, brisk walks daily to kick her metabolism into gear and help her get into good condition again. Do not quit because the weather is not good. Bad weather requires the expenditure of more caloric energy on the part of the dog and will help reduce the weight. When she's lost some weight and in better shape, increase the length of the walks. Put her food bowl down for a specified length of time and no longer. Ensure she can't get to the other dogs' food. About once every five to ten days, don't feed her for 24 hours. This will help maintain a healthy gut, make her less picky about what food she does get, and mimics nature. Food is NOT guaranteed in nature. Cut out ALL treats and if you do return to giving them, do so with caution and reduction of food at feeding time to compensate for the calories in the treats. Both you and your dog will be healthier if you do all of this.

There is a HUGE difference between a healthy dog and a fit dog. Your goal, if you love her, should be to have a healthy, fit dog.

Chapter  5

His Finest Hour

We were grouped under the trees for shade as the day was growing uncomfortably warm. I counted the dogs in front of me and realized that a lady who had called the day before had not yet arrived.

It wasn't a surprise; I lived out in the country and usually on their first class clients showed up incredibly early, as they were nervous about finding the place, or they were incredibly late, having gotten lost. I decided to wait a few more minutes before starting class.

While getting to my place wasn't really difficult, I had learned to give very specific instructions, right down to the eighth of the mile, and describe the types of roads on which people would be traveling. Too often I'd receive calls and a forlorn voice would wail, "I turned on a dirt road, but I can't find you."

"Can you give me some idea of where you are? What does it look like?" I'd query.

My very rural area was devoid of major landmarks and it made it difficult for my mental GPS to help them get back to the right place if I couldn't get a fix on them. Many times I, or an obliging person from class, had to drive a few miles in order to lead the lost owner to class.

Couple all this with the fact that once the person turned onto my road there was almost three miles of nothing, not a house or a telephone pole, nothing, and it made first-timers nervous, often causing them to turn around thinking they weren't on the right road.

The last sign of civilization was the cattle guard at the frontage road turn-off and a yellow sign full of bullet holes which read "Range Cattle." After that it was coolies and grassland, dotted by the occasional mule deer or pronghorn. Both the cattle guard and sign were the two primary identifying markers I used in describing how to reach the house. I often warned clients if they didn't see these two things, they were on the wrong road.

I was just about to announce that we'd wait five more minutes before beginning when my property's early warning system kicked into gear. A couple of dogs in the kennel stood up, turned toward the front gate and a few began to bark. Instantly, they all chimed in and the din was incredible. I issued a high, sharp whistle and all went quiet.

"Wow, my dogs won't shut up like that," the amazement in the woman's voice was clear.

"Sure they will," I laughed without turning. "You just need to be in charge."

"No one can sneak onto this place, can they?" Alan calmed his Spaniel and his voice filled with amusement as he joked, "Great security system."

"I can't see the gate for the trees, but the dogs always act as a doorbell. It gives me a chance to get it together before the person reaches the house." I smiled at him. "It also means that my kids, when they were teenagers, could never sneak in late. They hated that." The group laughed.

We all watched as two cars crawled up the long drive, parked and emptied themselves of dogs and owners as a third began to make its way toward us up the hill.

"Look at how big Jack has gotten since the last class," someone behind me gasped. Heads turned to look at the Old English sheepdog who the week before had looked like a puppy, but now had seemed to treble in size in only a few, short days.

This was a friendly, easy-going bunch of people and even though they hadn't known each other in the beginning, some fast friendships had developed and the owners took a keen interest in each other's dogs, their improvement and their class-mates' lives in general. It made for a great feeling all around.

I quickly assessed Jack, the Old English, and Midge, the Bichon, as they approached the group. Walking next to each other, both dogs were building up excitement and leaning into their leashes as if they were long-standing partners on an Iditarod sled team. Their owners were desperately attempting to put on the brakes as they were dragged into class.

"Whoa!" I quickly made my way to the pair of young dogs. "Take these two back over there, please," I made a motion in the general direction of the cars, "and start again. Don't let them learn to come to class like that. Manners. You need to insist on manners." Jack and Midge's owners gave me guilty smiles and retreated to where the pulling had begun. Making their dogs sit and calm down, they watched as an Amazon made her stately way past them.

At five feet nine inches I had always

been considered fairly tall, but this woman dwarfed even the men in the class. It wasn't often I stared at the second button on a person's shirt, but this woman made me feel small. She towered a full six foot three inches, was a perfectly proportioned, rock-solid 250 plus pounds, and had nothing with her. Even the dogs were shooting her curious glances.

"Hi." I didn't quite know how to greet her. Was she lost? Had she followed one of the people through the gate, as sometimes happened, hoping for directions? If she was here for dog class, where was the dog? I didn't want to make an idiot of myself, so I simply smiled and waited.

"Hi, I'm Dory." Her smile was beautiful, confident and relaxed, not what I normally saw on dog owners' faces. "My dog's name is Kit?" I must have had a very blank look as she continued, "I called yesterday... he won't sit or stay?"

"Oh, right," I sounded a little bemused, even to myself. "Where is he?"

"Here." Her infectious laugh floated through the group as she reached into the kangaroo pocket on the front of her sweatshirt and removed the tiniest dog I had ever seen. It fit in the palm of her hand with room to spare. Curiosity sped through the group like wildfire and they all pushed forward to get a glimpse of what she held.

Sitting, for the entire world like a king

on a throne greeting an adoring multitude, was a teacup Pomeranian. He couldn't have been much more than four pounds and about six inches tall, but his personality was gigantic. He had charisma, he radiated happiness and he was just about the most beguiling puppy I had ever seen. He was trouble, with a capital "T".

A perfect musical chorus of oohs and ahhs, which would have turned the Mormon Tabernacle Choir green with envy, swelled as all voices chimed in and they gazed at the miniature pup. Not one person in the group remained unaffected by the small dog.

"My goodness, don't put him down, we'll never find him in the grass," laughed one woman.

"He'll give an entirely new meaning to 'careful where you step'," joked Mark, a burly man with a seven month-old mastiff.

I fought the urge to take the little monster from Dory's hand and cuddle him. And little monster he was. I could see it in his eyes. He knew he had power over the weak humans around him. He knew he could bend us to his will. He knew that his diminutive size, his dandelion-fluff coat of reddish-gold and his large, shining dark brown eyes had the same effect on us as Kryptonite on Superman. We were powerless in his presence and he reveled at his hold over us.

"He's only a dog, keep telling yourself that," I mentally exhorted myself. "Get a grip, you're a professional." Yep, and so was the dog. He could have given charm lessons to the best of them. Already he was working his magic as hands materialized out of thin air in order to pet him.

Dory, the experienced hand-maiden to this diminutive god, stood patiently waiting for the adoration to wind down and for Kit to indicate what she should do next. Then I saw it; Kit turned his head slightly, gave her a sidelong glance, and I swear, infinitesimally and regally bowed his head, and in response to this unspoken communication Dory began to kneel in order to place him on the ground.

"Wait," I commanded. Dory froze in a half-kneeling pose and Kit shot me a look of unadulterated irritation which clearly said, 'How dare you interrupt the royal descent."

"What are you using for a leash?" This question clearly confused Dory.

"Leash?"

"Yeah, leash. What do you use?" I had a nasty image of this tiny tyrant dashing off into the hinterlands of my forty acres and my spending many panicked hours looking for him.

"I don't use a leash." I must have had a fairly stupid look on my face as she continued, "I offer him a treat when I need to catch him."

"Does it work?" I asked in astonishment.

"Sometimes..."

"What about when it doesn't?"

"Well, then, I just sit down and wait for him to come to me." She had the grace to look embarrassed.

Telling her to hang on, I dashed into the house and retrieved the lightest-weight leash in my arsenal. I returned, and creating a loop at the end of the leash, slipped it over Kit's head and indicated that Dory could now put him on the ground.

The second Kit's feet touched earth he took off at high speed. This was obviously a scenario to which he'd become accustomed. This time, however, he hit the end of the leash and pulled up short.

Kit froze in place. Slowly, in the tradition of silent screen comics, he turned, viewed the offending restraint and then threw a full-blown hissy-fit. If a small country could have harnessed that temper-tantrum it would have had no energy problems for a decade. (Over the next two hours I learned that it was also a renewable resource.)

As I watched Kit in his fury I could only be thankful that he was small or I would have had a very difficult time controlling him. He threw himself around like a landed trout. Flipping this way and that, rolling on the ground, leaping in the air, pulling backwards and then rushing madly forwards with a growl meant to intimidate me, he fought the leash for all he was worth.

The dogs in class looked on in utter disbelief. A few had awe written plainly on their faces. Chloe, the mastiff who was a full one-hundred-sixty-five pounds, stood up and back-pedaled rapidly to stay out of reach of the whirling dervish in front of her. Hiding behind her owner she trembled, using Mark as a shield against this unknown threat.

Without a pause for breath Kit suddenly changed tactics and viciously snared a length of the webbing between his teeth and began to gnaw, growl and rapidly whip his head from side to side in the manner of a master hunter intent on snapping the neck of his prey. I let loose with a serious and commanding correction sound and Kit went still.

The dog's glare of defiance began at my feet and slowly worked its way up until at last, his brown eyes, which a short time before I had believed to be warm and friendly, skewered me, narrowed imperceptibly and then his gaze, never breaking mine, hardened into a look of utter contempt. If looks could have killed I would have dropped where I stood. I would have turned to a pillar of stone. I would have ex-

perienced immolation. Kit's look indicated
that he'd be only too happy to watch me suffer all three. With premeditated disgust Kit
spat out the leash, turned his back on me
and sat down, dismissing my existence.
I couldn't help it, I had to laugh. It
wasn't often I was offered such an open
challenge, a throwing of a gauntlet, particularly from a dog that clearly refused to
acknowledge that his size was against him.
I had to admire this dog. He had issued a
declaration of war and he meant to have it
taken seriously.

"I'm going to work with Kit for a while,
Dory. Why don't you just watch and if you
have any questions, feel free to jump in and
ask them." I had no intention of letting Kit
get the upper hand. He might only weigh
four pounds, but he was the living embodiment of the old adage, "It's not the size of
the dog in the fight, but the size of the fight
in the dog." Dory didn't have a clue as to
what was happening and it was clear Kit
had trained her well to meet his demands
without hesitation.

I assigned various skills to be worked
on by different dogs. I paired up a few, sent
one or two to an enclosed area where owners could build confidence as they worked
off-leash and reminded all to stay within
view so I might offer suggestions, head off
problems and correct mistakes quickly.
The group dispersed more quietly than I'd

ever seen, no one was laughing or joking as they normally did. Many gave last looks at us as they headed off with their dogs reluctantly following. If you'd asked me right then, I would have told you all the dogs in class were placing bets on the outcome of the battle of wills which was to take place. I'd also tell you that their bets were evenly split between Kit and me at that moment.

"Dory, how old is Kit?" She looked a little shaky and I wanted to put her at ease.

"Four months."

Oh, Lord...I groaned inwardly. Only four months old, willful, smart and already a master at manipulation, if Kit had weighed another ten pounds this would be a breeze. But, I knew that my biggest obstacle would be overcoming the built-in, human psychological response.

"Dory, you need to understand that for a dog to accept you as the leader, it must respect you. To respect you they need to believe that you make the rules and enforce them. To establish and enforce those rules you need to communicate clearly what it is you expect in the way of behavior and what happens if the dog ignores you, your commands or your rules. You need to be clear in your communication, fair in your discipline, and firm in your expectations." Kit was still seated with his back to me as if I didn't exist.

"All I want is for him to sit when he's told and stay there." Her tone was pleading and I realized she was overcome by Kit's outburst. It was a side of him she'd never seen and for which she was unprepared. It had also been hard for her to watch as she hadn't viewed it as a refusal to accept me as a leader, but as a panicked dog fearfully trying to get free.

"I know. But, you need to understand that Kit doesn't see any reason to follow your rules because HE'S in charge. You follow HIS rules. He's trained you." At this exact moment, as if in response to my divulging a state secret, Kit shot a withering glance over his shoulder in my direction, stood, and with a public relation spin that only a master politician could appreciate, launched himself at Dory as if he'd been grossly abused and she was his haven in this cruel world.

Before Dory had a chance to respond, I reeled in the leash and reseated the Machiavellian canine at my feet. His explosion was instantaneous and nuclear in its power. It was the Susan and Kit re-enactment of the dining room scene from the Helen Keller movie. Kit broke and made a run for it; I grabbed him, hauled him back and made him sit in place. I stopped counting at his seventeenth attempt. Dory stood mute and watched.

Kit finally gave in and held a sit with

much sulking and a very bad attitude. I could tell he was planning his next move and kept a wary eye on him as I went on to explain an important point to Dory.

"Human's are psychologically hard-wired to protect, comfort and take care of small living creatures with big eyes. This ensures our off-spring the greatest chance for survival. If we didn't have this need built-in and we ever had an inkling of what they'd become in their teens, we'd probably leave the baby on a rock in winter and the human race would die out." Dory saw the humor in that and relaxed as she began to laugh.

"The problem is that your dog fits the physical profile which plays on our psychological weak point. You respond to Kit's size by feeling like you need to care for him, carry him, do for him, and protect him, when he can actually do quite a bit for himself." I could see I had her attention and continued. "If he lived with other dogs, they'd expect quite a bit from him at this time in his life. As it is, we compound our psychological weakness with a numerical one – we correlate his age of four months to human development at the same stage." Dory's eyebrows raised and I could see my point had hit home.

"Because of accelerated maturation on the part of the dog, a shorter life span, and Nature's endowing it with earlier self-sufficiency in many areas for basic survival, we can't look at a four month old dog as equivalent to a four month old baby. We need to get that out of our heads."

"What are they equivalent to then?" she questioned.

"Oh, a dog Kit's age is closer to a seven or eight year old human."

"What?" Her entire faced registered disbelief.

"Yep, and we have certain standards and skills we expect eight year olds to be able to reach and maintain. You wouldn't let a child get to that age without having taught rules and social behavior skills, so you shouldn't let your dog do it, either."

Kip chose this moment to put his plan into action. If flight had failed, and resistance had failed, he was now fully prepared to engage in frontal assault. He turned and tried to sink his teeth into my ankle.

It was a combination of many years of reading and instantly reacting to dogs, as well as dumb luck, which foiled his attempt to draw blood. I must have felt a change in the leash, seen something from the corner of my eye, felt a difference in the atmosphere, but whatever the case, I pulled my foot back quickly and his teeth only caught the fabric of my jeans. He was surprised that I hadn't quailed at his physical onslaught as so many others had. It had worked on vet techs, children he was tired of, even Dory herself when Kit was teaching her a lesson in how and when to leave him alone. In this case, however, he found himself jerked uncomfortably along with the fabric he'd managed to snag while my intolerance for biting rained down on him.

Lifting him from the ground I held him nose to nose with me and growled an aahht that had been known to make large dogs retreat. His eyes widened in surprise and he went limp in my hand. I stared at him for a few seconds longer and then lowered him back to the ground. I skewered him with a look that indicated he could choose to pursue this or let it go, his decision. He watched me briefly and then sat down. The battle was over, but the war was yet to be won.

For the remaining class time I worked with Dory to help her win her coup over the reigning monarch. It was slow going as Kit fought her every step of the way. By the end of the morning both of them were tired.

I watched the pair as they headed for the car. Dory was keeping a steady pace that could have easily been met by Kit, but he resisted every step of the way. It was amusing to watch Kit attempt to halt the imposing woman in her tracks as he lagged behind refusing to walk on the leash.

As they drove off down the drive Kit's head popped up in the rear window of the car and he stared malevolently at me until they were out of sight.

The next Saturday, Dory and Kit were amongst the first to arrive. Kit jumped excitedly from the back of the car and went absolutely still. His face registered his shock and dismay. "Not this again," it seemed to say.

With a mulish look he sat and refused to move. Dory corrected him and I was glad to see he gave in with little argument. Kit's face was an easy read and as he and his owner walked to the class area it was apparent that he was making plans. The second he saw me, however, his eyes took on a sly glint and his expression changed.

Suddenly he became joyous, bouncing and excited to see me. I raised an eyebrow in disbelief. I often told owners that dogs must try every trick in their bag before they came to believe that their human was in charge. In the case of Kit, he had one hundred tricks and he was absolutely positive that one of them would work on me and reseat him on his throne.

He expressed joy at seeing me again which knew no bounds. He greeted me as if I were his long-lost soul mate. I was the one human on the earth that understood him, loved him without bounds, the human who had been his owner through many previous lifetimes finally rejoined. I didn't believe him.

Dory and I stood discussing how the week had gone for her while Kit snuggled against my ankle and oozed contentment, joy and pleasure at my presence. He gazed with complete adoration and he made certain our physical contact was unbroken as he lay across the top of my shoe.

"I thought he only did that with me," Dory sounded a little hurt as she looked down at the small pup.

"Hmm....Possession is nine-tenths of the law," my tone wary as I waited for Kit's next move.

At that moment Mark and Chloe walked up. The big mastiff pup, still somewhat ungainly within herself, caught sight of her nemesis and reared back in panic. Kit, totally unfazed, watched as Chloe effortlessly dragged Mark backwards a good ten feet in order to maintain distance from the danger that lay at my feet.

"Mark, anchor that leash around that fence post, Chloe needs to meet Kit and get over this fear," I told the struggling man.

"Kit...walk." Without hesitation Kit fell in beside me and calmly approached Chloe whose entire body was poised for flight. The closer Kit and I got, the wider Chloe's eyes became.

I stopped Kit about three feet from the big dog in order to allow her time to calm down, assess the situation and see that she was in no danger. Chloe, retreating to the end of her leash, was putting immense pressure on the post and I hoped it wouldn't give way.

When nothing happened, Chloe began to relax. Kit maintained perfect behavior and in a very short time Chloe moved forward to investigate the tiny dog. Kit posed regally, allowing the young mastiff to sniff uninterrupted. Finally, at some unspoken communication between the two dogs, Kit slowly turned and quietly licked Chloe's nose. She jerked her head back and sneezed violently. We all laughed with delight and then watched as the giant dog lay down and carefully tried to engage Kit in a game of play. The gentleness of the big dogs always amazed me and Chloe was no exception.

I gave Mark instructions for the day's work and he and Chloe moved off together. Kit was far from happy. Pulling and barking on the leash he tried to follow. I uttered a correction and he shot me a venomous look. The war had resumed.

Dory struggled all during class to get control over Kit. He had the boundless energy of the small dog and he used every ounce of it in thwarting the desires of his owner. After a fifteen minute battle to make Kit hold a sit Dory had lost all confidence in her ability to teach her dog. It was imperative that I rebuild her belief in her skills, and quickly, or Kit would regain control of their relationship.

I gave a long, piercing whistle and waited as everyone regrouped around me. It was time for an object lesson which would benefit everyone, not merely Kit and Dory.

"I want everyone to pass his leash and dog to the person on your right." Owners looked at each other in disbelief. Hesitantly leashes began to trade hands. People were watching their new charges with trepidation.

"You have only one goal, that's to make the dog you're handling follow the behavioral-obedience rules you've been taught. Let's start with you." I pointed to a young man now in charge of an easy-going Chesapeake Bay retriever named Brat, and motioned him to begin.

The pair began to walk and within a very short time was doing very well. Brat's owner watched in amazement.

"Why doesn't he behave that well with me?" Her voice was a combination of envy, hurt and frustration.

"Just wait and watch," I replied patiently.

All twelve people successfully walked their "new" dogs without problems. The dogs, for the most part, were well behaved and with the one or two that tried to act out, the person quickly corrected it and continued on uninterrupted. Even Kit managed to walk without a display and listened well.

"Can anyone tell me why you managed to walk an unknown dog without complications, when you have problems with your pet?" I questioned. I was met with silence and blank faces.

"It's because," I continued, "You are not emotionally invested in the dog. You aren't worried about what other people think of you, of your dog, or its behavior. You are not embarrassed or nervous. The dog is not picking up insecure or negative emotional feedback and so it doesn't react inappropriately. If you'd communicate that same confidence to your own dog you'd have a lot less problems." I had everyone reclaim their dogs and sent them out to work. There was a difference in the air; it was a palpable feeling of change and the dogs knew it, too.

Dory, having just successfully walked a very active lab mix, confidently took control of Kit and set off. The change was amazing. Dory returned and told me that she felt that Kit had offered little resistance and actually seemed to be relieved that she was in charge. I was pleased. Kit seemed to understand that he had lost this particular battle and capitulated gracefully.

Unlike the previous two weeks, I heard little from Dory between classes. I took that as a good sign and when the third Saturday rolled around I looked forward to seeing how much ground Dory had gained.

She and Kit came to class happy, relaxed and seemed pleased with their new relationship. It was clear that Kit now respected her, her commands and was at ease with the transfer of power. I thought it time to work on teaching him to come when called.

This had been a big problem which was still worrying Dory. Kit did well in every other area, but once free from her physical control he simply would not come when called. I decided since many dogs were ready to work on either an off-leash down, a long down or a come, it would be best to do it in a group setting. I gathered everyone together.

When it was Kit's turn to work on come, I had to administer a couple of corrections to make him understand I was deadly serious about his not moving until called. I backed away and called him to come. He made a small movement in my direction, and then stopped. His face said it all, "Oh, no....this is a test. I won't fall for it. I'm staying right here, thank you."

"It's OK, Kit. Come." I spread my arms wide in an inviting gesture. The small dog was thinking so hard you could smell the gears burning. "Come." I repeated. Hesitantly he took a step forward.

"That's right, atta boy. Come." I made certain I sounded pleased. Kit cautiously made his way across the ten feet which separated us until he sank into a sit at my feet.

For the very first time since he'd begun class I petted the tiny dynamo with affection. "Good come, Kit. Good come!" I picked him up and held him close as I gave him a hug of pleasure, then I put him on the ground again and smiled at him.

Kit sat stunned with a shocked look on his face. It was clear what he was thinking. "If that's all it takes to make you happy, why didn't you say so earlier?" I laughed, I just couldn't help it.

I trusted this dog completely now and in reward for his behavior I released him to play for a moment. "Play, Kit," and I waved my hand. His small head cocked at an angle, he gave me a quizzical look. "Go on, play," I repeated.

With his head thrown up and tail held high, his dandelion-fluff coat of reddish-gold rippling, his large, dark brown eyes shining, the tiny super nova of joy sped around the yard. Each and every person laughed, no one was immune, I least of all. It is a rare thing to witness such pure and unadulterated joy. It is one of the reasons I love working dogs so much.

Kit made a final circle and streaked straight to me stopping and sitting a few inches away. His gaze began at my feet and slowly worked its way up until at last, his brown eyes, brimming with laughter, friendship and pleasure met mine. The war was over.

Kit, Teacup Pomeranian, age 4 months

Kit, at such a young age, had very few behavioral problems, but the one he had was well on its way to being firmly established. Had his owner not begun obedience classes, that one problem would have created many more. Dory had endowed him with the role of leader.

Dory unintentionally treated Kit, due to his size, as if he were a helpless, newborn human child and created a world in which he was kept from learning and mastering the basic skills of any dog – walking, following rules, doing for himself and developing a respect for her as his leader.

This small dog was willful and smart. In this case many would term the pup as "stubborn," but willful is more accurate. That will, often seen in sporting, hunting and herding dogs, rises to challenges with the intent and determination to overcome an obstacle. It is what keeps these dogs from giving in when faced with odds which are against them and allows them, as in the case of a stock dog, to control groups of animals many times their size through sheer determination and brains. The goal with dogs such as these is to not teach in a manner which the dog learns to challenge the human leader's authority.

Dory needed to learn to control her human responses to Kit's size. She needed to learn how to insist the pup respect her, her demands and expectations for his behavior. She had to balance the developing pup's need to explore his world in order to develop his physical skills; his emotional needs which would continue to help him remain stable; and his social skills which would teach him to respect her and still behave in an acceptable manner in general during this critical period of the first six months of his life.

Dory's failing was that of so many people who have small dogs and of puppy owners in general. When a pup misbehaves or challenges the human's authority, the owner simply picks the dog up, or removes it from the problem area, and stops it from its actions instead of correcting the misbehavior. He may pet the dog to calm it down. This actually reinforces the incorrect behavior and the dog redoubles its efforts in the wrong behavior the next time the opportunity presents itself, thinking this is how it's expected to behave in this type of situation.

The largest challenge was not Kit, but Dory. She had to accept the fact that her dog, regardless of its size, was not helpless, not incapable, and not totally dependent on her for everything. Dory had to be made to see that by loving Kit, both physically and emotionally, without establishing set rules of behavior, Kit interpreted this to mean she was of lesser status and groveling for his approval. Since it was only the two of them, Kit took the leadership position.

Once Dory realized that she could teach Kit good behavior that had nothing to do with his size, that it didn't require the severe method of choke chains or the bribery of treats, she was able to reclaim the mantle of leader and both she and Kit were better for it.

Questions & Answers

Q: "You always go on and on about discipline, making the dog mind, doing what you want. You tell people not to give treats, not to pet or tell the dog how good it is each time it does something right. My dogs are my babies and I would do anything to make them happy-something YOU don't seem to do or understand. What is it with you???? I don't think you like dogs very much."

A: Ironically it is the dogs' side I take in all issues. I believe that it is our responsibility as humans to do the changing in order to give the dog an opportunity to shine.

I'm not sure if the dislike/anger coming through is due to the fact that I am not overly fond of current training methods, or if it is because I am not an advocate for behaving bountifully at the dogs' expense.

I DO know that in today's society many of the loudest and vociferous people are loath to discipline children and dogs, hold themselves or their children/dogs to a level of acceptable behavior, and make every excuse under the sun for their actions. Many try to force anyone who does have expectations of behavior into a corner with threats of legal action, or bad-mouth them claiming they're destroying the child's/dog's self-esteem, and yet, these same people are the first in line to scream for laws that govern behavior in those with whom they don't agree. The attitude clearly points the direction that humans are heading when it comes to inter-personal/intra-species relationships; make it sweet, make it nice, let someone else do the dirty work and, above all, no conflicts or confrontations. I call it, "The Shirley Temple Syndrome."

My antennae go up when an owner demands only "sweetness and light" (wholly positive) or choke-chain based training methods. Why? I can only believe the individual has chosen one of these forms on a strictly personal basis and cannot, or will not, see how he, personally, both affects and effects the dog. Yet, no one ever questions the validity or efficacy of either of these training methods.

Anyone who has had a relationship

of any kind, who has watched ducks, dogs, elephants or humans knows that there is conflict, dominance, leadership, subjugation, manipulation, love, comfort, grief and a myriad of other emotions that play out within the complex interaction. It varies from relationship to relationship, but it exists. Mr. Cesar Millan is correct when he states, "All animals follow dominant leaders, not lovable leaders." This is because we look to the strong for emotional and physical security. Those who are unsure in time of trouble, that cannot provide in times of need, are unable to protect in times of danger don't instill a lot of hope or trust in us.

In all my years working dogs the biggest complaint against me used to be that I allowed people to be affectionate with their dogs-but, more recently, that I do not encourage clients to praise consistently. The pendulum will never stay inert. The Greeks stated it best, "Nothing in excess, everything in moderation". I see nothing wrong with affection...but, the new, totally positive training approaches don't work either. Dogs can adapt to new things quickly, but habits take time. Science itself, and scientists, have stated that empirical evidence and incontrovertible proof is the only thing they believe, which of course is the basis for behavioral studies...the problem with THAT is it doesn't take into account the individual, both dog and human, that skews the process mentally, emotionally and now genetically with selectively or poorly bred dogs.

It is claimed that dogs have been selectively bred for 15,000 or more years to live with people. I found this to be a bit skewed and somewhat inaccurate. Recent DNA studies show that dogs have only been bred as specific breeds for less than 200 years. Prior to that, they were bred for traits, like to like, in order to produce dogs that could be used for a specific talent and characteristic. Living with people, as we see it today, was truly low on the list. HUNTING FOR people was the first and most important trait. The only other trait that needed to be with that was a temperament that would take commands. Most of those dogs, as still evidenced by today's Pariah dogs of India and the New Guinea Singing Dog, were either kept securely tied or allowed to roam at will and fend for themselves with little human interaction until such time as the dog's talents were needed. The dogs were, and for the most part still are, NOT brought into the family and made members such as we do today. They definitely were NOT humanized as we see in America.

To constantly praise, with words, food or touch, is to demean, lessen and dilute its impact. To consistently use choke chains or other harsh methods is to break the ability to think, the will, and spirit and crush the individuality of the dog.

ALL methods of written, video and cookie-cutter training are generalized for public consumption. It simply will not work. Their problem is that they cannot moderate tone, touch, or response in the individual; they can merely make a "written in stone" statement. The owners have a direct responsibility for, and impact on, the behavior of their dogs—as do their children, spouses and families—like it or not. I have yet to see training methods which believe as I do; the owner has some common sense, feelings and knowledge of his dog.

Owners must be given some leeway in which to interact with their pet. However, any time you get a formulaic training method you get iron-clad do and don't statements because owners go overboard in both directions. I really think if you give them info and trust them they will modify what you say and the result will be a good relationship with good behavior from both dog and owner.

I try very hard to give general ideas which work because dogs have shown them to work...not scientists, not behaviorists who, as in the case of one dog park aggression study, spent 10 minutes per hour, four hours per day over four days recording behavior of dogs in dog parks and then wrote a study on aggressive behavior, or other limited time studies which were then turned into the "Sermon on the Mount" of dog behavior.

As for the common comparison of dogs/ wolves, it has been shown that wolves have a much more cohesive, structured social system which people attempt to translate into hierarchical behavior. This does not hold exactly true for dogs that are by nature more separatist-behaviorally inclined. The newest theory out is that dogs developed off the branch of wolf that was inclined to be a loner and to a large extent outside the pack and was thus more of a scavenger behind man. This may have been the off-color wolf which has been physically, socially and psychologically shunned and driven out by aggressive, forceful means by the pack.

I can't comment on that—I wasn't living at that time of genetic separation some 100,000 years ago (evidence obtained by sequencing mitochondrial DNA of 67 dog breeds and wolves from 27 locations –Vita et al., 1997). However, I do believe that science omits the important emotional aspect of the dog and behaviorists want to over-humanize the viewable physical and ocular actions. I sit more in the middle...there are behaviors which are endemic to all dogs, but one must take into account the individual emotional and environmental factors of the individual dog being worked.

The real problem here is the human...each person brings to his dog and its training personality conflicts, strengths, weaknesses, intelligence (both mental and native), adaptability, knowledge and willingness. The trainer must attempt to bring out the best in both the dogs and humans while the world expects perfectly behaved dogs and vilifies any trainer who fails to buy into a current, popular mindset 100%.

Many years ago, Ray Hunt, the 'Horse Whisperer', who ultimately worked Queen E's horses successfully, showed that there is a balance between sciences, nature and intimately acquired atavistic knowledge. Scientist and behaviorist denounced him at the time; some years later they collected enough info to support what he had been saying as to how horses think, act and behave. Hunt has often said, and I whole heartedly agree, "I didn't invent this method, nature and the horse has and it has worked well forever. I'm simply trying to translate what the horses taught me into something that you can understand and help you put into use for yourself and your horse. It's not the only way to do this, it's simply one way." The latter part of his statement simply meant that there was a myriad of training methods out there, but he felt most comfortable with his and felt both he and his horses were pleased with the results and their resulting relationship(s). He, and others like I, saw immense changes in incredibly short time spans with little or no stress on the animal as applied to behavior. To turn those changes into habit, however, requires time and consistent, repetitive handling and structure.

The basics are this, dogs have never lived in a consistently aggression-free positive zone, they have never lived in a consistently punitive zone, they don't behave towards one another excessively in either direction, they don't over quantify emotions, they don't carry forward guilt or emotional baggage, they engage in exercise on a regular, fairly high level which lowers stress and builds social, emotional and physical bonds...only when in contact with humans do we see any of this fall apart or be co-opted into our frame of reference with no thought as to the true dog.

So, with all that said...who really needs to do the most amount of behavioral changing to elicit the best responses consistently and offer the most balanced emotional and behavioral life? To me this is an easy answer...the human.

Chapter 6

Guess Who's Coming to Dinner?

"I gave your card to Jim and Betsy Johnson. They have the dog from hell and I told them you'd be able to help them." Tom was rolling up the sleeve of his shirt, exposing his forearm, as he leaned against the door of his truck.

"Geez, Tom, what happened?" I was aghast at the myriad of scabs which covered him from elbow to wrist.

"Mack, that's what happened." Tom swiveled his arm this way and that, up and down, giving me a good look at the road map of scratches, bites and scabbing which covered the entire lower portion of his left arm. Lowering his sleeve and buttoning the cuff, he continued, "Jim's a friend of mine, we hunt, do some business together, and have known each other for a long time, and his wife got a puppy a few months ago..."

"A puppy did that?" I interrupted him in surprise.

"Yeah, he's a Rhodesian ridgeback and he bites, scratches, crawls all over you – he's out of control. So, I gave your name to Betsy and told her to give you a call." He climbed into the truck, leaned out of the window and said, "They own a business and house in Virginia, and houses in a couple of other places. I don't know which place they'd need you to come to, but I sure hope you'll consider taking the dog on, he's only going to get worse." He put the truck in reverse, gave me a wave, and headed down the drive.

I turned and walked slowly to the house. I had met Tom and his wife as clients, but we'd become friends, and I considered them both wonderful people. We had a lot in common, and what we didn't share in the way of views was small and of no consequence. Their dog, Boss, had been a tough pup, but they had gotten a handle on him early and not allowed his behavior to develop into problems. The dog was admired by all who met him now, so considering what Tom had faced with Boss, if he said Mack was out-of-control I could only imagine how bad the dog must be.

Life went on and my schedule of working other people's dogs lightened. Summer slipped into fall and the leaves began to change as the days took on a special, golden light. It was a magical time and I had the rare opportunity to work my dogs on my livestock as often and for as long as we wanted. As much as I derived satisfaction from helping others correct the problems their dogs faced, I truly loved the ease with which my group all functioned and the camaraderie my dogs and I shared. It was a nice break.

It suddenly came to an abrupt end and my schedule was crammed with names of people in need of help. It was mid-September and I was already booked, without a break, until the end of October.

It was nine o'clock at night and I had just walked in the door after a long day filled with unruly dogs only to be greeted by the phone's insistent ringing. I contemplated it as one would the discovery of a rattlesnake in the room – with a great deal of fear and an overwhelming urge to run. Don't answer it, was my immediate thought, but with an aged mother in another state and children spread across the world that was not an option. I picked it up.

"This is Susan."

"Hi, this is Betsy Johnson and Tom

Miles gave me your name and said I should call you. I have a problem with my dog." The accent was not Virginian, just a pleasant, business-like tone with no hint of worry.

"Oh, right. I remember him telling me you might call," I was a little surprised as it had been almost a month since Tom and I had spoken and I'd figured that the Johnsons had found local help for their dog problem. "How are you?"

"Awful. I don't know what Tom told you about Mack, but he's uncontrollable," the voice was no longer pleasant, but fraught with stress and exasperation. "We have our own business and we meet with our clients and board members in our house. Mack has made that impossible for us by his behavior. I'm doing something wrong with him and I don't know what it is. Tom said you can fix any dog. I need to know if I can get you to come down here and work on Mack before my husband makes me give him away."

"Where's here?" I couldn't help but like this woman, she was honest, straight to the point and made no excuses for her dog's behavior. It almost guaranteed that the human portion of the equation, which was always the hardest part, would in this case, be easy.

"I'm in Virginia. I'll be here another week and then we'll be in our place in Colorado and after that, New Mexico." I was scribbling madly as I took down the information and dates. After much conversation we finally settled on meeting in New Mexico during the last week of October and I promised I'd get back to her with flight information so that she could pick me up at the airport. I then dragged myself through the evening chores and headed for bed.

Within a couple of days I had the travel arrangements settled and had e-mailed Betsy my itinerary. I'm not a fan of the Internet, but when it comes to booking flights the computer beats the telephone, hands down. It's also is a boon to communications as it allows me to send messages at ungodly hours that most people refuse to recognize as being on the clock.

I then turned my attention to making sure my dogs were taken care of in my absence, not an easy task with seven dogs, no near neighbors, no television reception, and thirty miles from the nearest McDonald's. People that could handle all of that with aplomb were a rare commodity, even in the ranching community.

Because neither the Johnsons nor I lived in communities that were top destination spots, I was required to change planes several times in order to reach the small New Mexico town closest to their home. It gave me plenty of opportunity to read and think about how I wanted to work Mack in the limited time I had with him.

I called Betsy as I got ready to board the last plane and warned her, "I should be there in about an hour."

"We're about forty minutes from the airport," she said excitedly. "Can I bring Mack with me?"

"Sure. I can't wait to meet him." I rang off as I heard the final boarding call and made my way to the gate.

Exiting the airport's baggage area doors I looked for the white SUV Betsy told me she'd be driving. Appearing out of nowhere on my left was a woman who closely matched my height. She was smiling warmly, wore jeans and a button-down shirt and looked as down-to-earth and friendly as she had sounded on the phone.

"Susan?"

"Betsy, how are you?"

"Fine, how was your flight?" She led the way to the vehicle and popped open the rear. I was suddenly greeted by a rocking dog crate and a dark, golden head peering from behind the metal-grating door.

"Good. Boring." I threw my bag in the SUV. "Is that Mack?"

"Yes," she proudly replied. "You sit in the front. This is John, one of our board members, he's down doing some work this week, he agreed to drive so I could control Mack and we could talk."

I flinched inwardly; "control" was not

a word one liked to hear at almost ten at night, especially after twelve hours of flying and the prospect of another hour with a dog that was young, strong, and full of energy. Particularly as it pertained to a dog which had left visible signs of its oral fixation all over the forearm of my friend.

As we pulled away from the curb, Betsy reached over the back seat and released Mack from his crate. He exploded into her lap, licking, wiggling and then quickly turning his attention to John, who was driving, and then me. He was forty-odd pounds of steel and muscle with energy to spare and, thank God, a good temperament. He was friendly, full of joy, agile and didn't have a self-controlled bone in his constantly moving body. A young, excited Rhodesian ridgeback in a small, dark, contained space – thank God we were in margarita country.

Mack was standing with his front paws on the console between the seats, his head a metronome as he nudged first John, then me. He filled the entire middle section of the car, blocking any hope of a view in the mirror by John or my seeing Betsy while we attempted to talk. His tail, an uncontrolled cudgel, rhythmically slapped his owner's shoulder, face and body as she vainly held her hands up in a defensive gesture trying to protect herself and pleading, "Mack, sit...Mack...Ouch, stop it, Mack!...Sit...Get down. Are you...Mack, sit down, NOW!...

hungry? Mack, no!...Would you like us... Mack, get off that...to stop someplace and ...Mack, don't. Sit....grab you something to eat?"

There was no way we would survive forty minutes of this. There was no way I would survive another two minutes. I reached back, collared Mack, gave him a tiny, quick, serious collar-scruff and said one word, "Aahht!" He became absolutely still as my eyes bored into him, then slowly he sank to the seat, quietly lying next to Betsy without moving.

Silence and calm were now the order of the day, but I didn't release my hold on his collar. In the strobe-like flashing of the street lights I had seen great intelligence in Mack's eyes and I wanted to be absolutely certain he understood there was a new sheriff in town. I meant business and could, and would, back my play.

"I'm alright, thanks. I ate on the plane." I maintained my hold of Mack's collar and the two of us continued to watch each other. Mack blinked first and his look telegraphed his thoughts and feelings. This was not how it was supposed to happen, he was supposed to greet the newcomer. Jump on her, lick her and chew on her. He was supposed to engage in a tug-of-war with her arm. He was unsure just what was happening and what I might do, so he erred on the side of caution and remained still on the seat next to Betsy.

"What's that sound you're making?" John radiated a combined feeling of disbelief and amusement.

"'Aahht?' Oh, it's a correction sound that dogs respond to and understand—something along the lines of a growl." I continued to stare at Mack who was longing to crawl onto Betsy's lap.

"Seems to work." John's tone spoke volumes. I felt the relief coming off him in waves. I could only imagine what he'd put up with for the past few days.

"This is great," Betsy's naturally buoyant personality was reasserting itself, but it was also feeding Mack's hyper personality and he began to struggle to, once again, defy the law of physics by putting two objects in a single space and sit on her lap.

"Mack...aahht." I warned and he immediately returned to his place beside Betsy.

We talked of trivial matters as we traveled back roads in the dark. I was hopelessly lost and finally gave up trying to keep track of inky landmarks. Suddenly we turned and came to a stop. Betsy reached for the door and Mack came to full alert, ready to jump from the car. Grabbing him quickly, I held on while she went to open the gate.

"He's a friendly dog," said John when

Betsy departed, "But he is a handful. The more you try to make him calm down, the worse he behaves. And he's strong; he can draw blood without meaning to." The car crawled through the gate and we waited for Betsy to climb back in. "Mack sits on the sofa, we sit on the floor."

"WHAT?!?" My astonishment knew no bounds at this pronouncement and I wasn't sure if he was serious.

"Yep, we're all sitting there and Mack gets up, walks all over us, pushes us around, finally, you just sit on the floor and let him have the sofa. It's easier that way."

With Betsy back in, we drove slowly through a landscape of mesquite bushes and little else. Suddenly the lights of the house shone at a distance. It was a welcoming sight.

"Betsy, don't let Mack out until I get a leash on him." I didn't want this dog thinking he could get away from me or that once back on home territory I had no power.

"I didn't bring one," she said a little worriedly.

"That's OK, I have one." Pulling it from my backpack I quickly slipped it over Mack's head.

John burst out laughing, "Most women travel with make-up. You're the first I've seen to pack a leash."

The instant the car was turned off

Mack readied himself to burst out the door and forget the ride he'd had to live through. Home. Freedom. Stupidity. "Aahht!" Frozen, poised for the escape leap as he heard my warning, he stood thinking, and thinking hard. I was beginning to really like this dog and I knew he'd be great to work with. His intelligence was keen, he was already trying to figure out just where to put me in his world and if I really carried the powers and abilities I was communicating. Instead of his original plan to explode from the vehicle and dash around madly, he opted for discretion and sat quietly in the back waiting for my next move. I called him over the seat and out the front door. With great control and nobility he exited the car and stood patiently by my side.

In the moth-induced flickering of the porch light I saw an older dog hoist himself up off deck and stiffly make his way toward us. He was a portly Labrador, his coal-black hair was beginning to grey around the muzzle and his tail waved sedately to and fro as he ambled in our direction. This was the quintessential old-time Lab, unflappable, low-key, good tempered, friendly, lie-by-the-fire, everyone's friend kind of dog.

"That's Bailey," Betsy's voice floated through the dark from the rear of the car. At the sight of Bailey advancing across the grass Mack reverted to his puppy antics.

His head lowered, his rear raised and he began panting and whining. Bailey deviated from his direct line approach and swung wide to stay out of Mack's reach.

"Do Bailey and Mack get along?"

"They used to," Betsy came to stand beside me and bent to pet Bailey who had strategically placed her between himself and the whining four month old pup. "Recently he and Mack have gotten into it quite a bit. I'm getting worried because Bailey's not as young as he once was and it seems like he's really fed-up with Mack. They'll be alright, and then suddenly Bailey just turns and nails Mack. It's going to end up with one of them getting hurt, and I think it'll be Bailey."

I'd had enough of the silly behavior taking place at the end of the leash and gave a serious correction growl. Mack came to an instantaneous halt and sat of his own accord. Bailey's ears went forward and his tail wagged faster. His liquid brown eyes took on an amused delight as he fell into a prancing step next to us as our small group raggedly made its way to the house.

John, carrying my bag, was in the lead and waited to open the front door. Betsy and Bailey followed companionably with Bailey doing the old dog bounce-of-joy the entire way. I trailed with Mack, who failed, but made a valiant attempt at self-control, at my side. I thanked John, but indicated he should go in as Mack and I had a little work to do before we joined the group again.

The two of us stood on the deck as I looked out over the dark landscape. Mack was utterly confused. He had always been the first to enter and now here he was sitting outside with a stranger. I could feel his angst. Finally, when I felt him calm down, we entered.

I slept deeply, but because of the time change found myself wide awake and staring at a dark window. By the time I finished my shower there were streaks of light in the sky and I tip-toed out to the kitchen to get a cup of coffee. I had been very grateful when told that Jim was an early riser and the coffee pot was on a timer set for 4 AM. I hated rummaging through people's cabinets to make coffee, a necessity for me in the morning.

As I rounded the corner into the kitchen all hell broke loose from the mud-room. Mack had heard my arrival and was ready to get out of his crate. He whined, pawed and by sheer excitement managed to move the crate by inches across the floor of the utility room and toward the kitchen door. Quickly, I shushed him and doctored a cup of coffee and then headed to let him out.

Standing in front of the crate which had begun rocking again I quietly corrected the frantic dog and waited. Mack was not stupid, the crate went silent and he calmed down. The second my hand touched the crate door, however, a ruckus resumed. Again I waited.

After about four tries Mack got the idea and remained well-behaved as I reached for the door clip. I slowly began to open it and Mack tried to explode outwards. Just as quickly I popped the grated door back in place. It took only two attempts and Mack settled back as I opened the door and waited for me to give the cue that he could come out. Intelligent dogs were a joy to work with, especially before my full complement of coffee.

A buffalo stampede could have passed more quietly than Mack making his way to the front door. I was relieved to see that Jim and Betsy's bedroom door was closed. Mack's morning ritual attempt to wake the couple by bounding in and exuberantly leaping between them was foiled. Within a couple of quiet corrections Mack caught on and sat inside the front door waiting for his release.

It was going to be hot, that much I could tell. The sky was clear and already the air was warm even though the sun was barely above the horizon. Mack prodigiously watered every bush, rock and deck post within fifty feet, and then made his way off for some privacy for his serious morning needs. I kept a wary eye on him as I had been regaled the evening before with stories of his walkabout tendencies.

Betsy wandered out and I saw that I had a companion in the worship of the morning coffee cult. Bailey, companionable and easy-going as ever, nudged my elbow and wandered off into the yard without waiting for a pat from me. The old dog sniffed and investigated at leisure as he weighed the merits of where it best to do his morning deeds. Wandering from this place to the next and then backtracking, as if to compare the relative interior designs of the different bathrooms, Bailey was in his own little world.

It was while the Lab's head was deep in a flowering bush that Mack caught sight of him. With a display of power and speed so necessary for survival on the savanna, the young dog made straight for his elder companion. I sprang to my feet, spilling coffee everywhere, and issued a loud, commanding correction. It was just enough to keep Mack from body-slamming poor old Bailey. As it was, Mack brushed by the black dog as he was raising his head in response to my voice with just enough contact to send him staggering. The agile pup made an abrupt turn and then another beeline for Bailey.

I saw it coming. Bailey saw it coming. Pair skaters couldn't have timed their reactions better. Just as Mack reached the irritated and interrupted old Lab, Bailey snapped at him with authoritative discipline and I let loose with a commanding "Aahhtt!" at exactly the same moment. Mack's ears went back flat against his head, his tail dropped between his legs and he scampered up on the deck to sit abashedly next to Betsy. Betsy had missed it all. She hadn't seen Mack's wind-up, or his pitch, and so he was normally able to complete his misbehavior with only Bailey correcting him. I knew, now, where the most amount of work lay. I had to bring Betsy up to speed or Mack would spiral further and further out of control until he was a menace. Not because he was a bad or aggressive dog, but because he had the ability, strength and determination to be the lord of creation in every encounter. It went with the breed.

For the remainder of the morning I worked with Betsy setting up teaching opportunities and lecturing to her about dogs in general, and Mack specifically. By lunch I could tell she was on overload and couldn't take in any more. I decided it was time for a walk with the Mack and his owner.

Betsy and I had been working nonstop on Mack and his behavior since the evening before and the walk was a great way to enjoy life, teach and release stress. As we ambled down the lane toward the gate I allowed Mack to roam free with only a gentle reminder to stick around. Betsy and I talked as I carried the loosely coiled leash in one hand. I was looking into the distance at a group of historic old buildings while Betsy told me their tale when I felt a tug on the leash. I swept my eyes downward and began to chuckle. There was Bailey, waddling along next to me, vainly trying to get his head into the loop as it dangled next to my thigh.

"Hey, old man, want to walk with us?" I slipped the leash on Bailey, thumped his side affectionately, gave him slack and spoke to his owner, "I think Bailey wants to join class."

Betsy's look of shock grew even more pronounced as Mack circled back and, taking in our comfortable trio, slid into the mix without any disturbance. He walked with great self-control next to Bailey and Betsy without any leash.

"I just can't believe this," Betsy's voice registered her surprise. "I can't get them to walk together without Mack creating chaos and here he is, without a leash and not bothering Bailey...and Bailey seems really happy."

"It's a pack thing. I'm in charge, Bailey's sure I won't let Mack become an idiot, and Mack is following the rules. Everyone's happy."

On the way back to the house I released both dogs to go roam, sniff and have fun without much guidance from me. Betsy was much improved and more relaxed, too.

With only three days in which to work with both Betsy and Mack we packed every moment as full as possible in the first day-and-a-half. Betsy and Jim both hunted birds so Mack needed to be calm around guns. The couple also had a skeet range which provided the perfect opportunity to acclimate the young pup, without undue stress, to the sounds of guns. He was introduced to an ever-changing group of visitors and so was in a position to learn quickly how to behave well and greet all people. These and other skills we worked on non-stop in order to establish Mack's base behavior. It was easier on Mack than on Betsy, and easier on her than on her husband Jim.

Jim truly liked and loved the dogs. A big man, with a full voice and personality to match, he came home each evening and burst through the door where he was met by the dogs, both oozing anticipation and joy, which he rewarded with a treat in the kitchen. Neither dog was expected to do anything other than be happy at his arrival in order to receive this wonderful evening boon.

I really liked Jim, and had from the moment we met, but this tradition was causing problems. It took a little convincing, on both Betsy's and my part, to get him to agree to make the dogs sit calmly and behave, which meant no more wild, pagan dances at the feet of the "Treat God" each evening. However, he gave in with good grace in order to help the dogs and they rewarded his largesse by still frolicking at the door, but sitting in the kitchen. The "Treat God" was satisfied.

One of Mack's problems was he was a counter-surfer. Put the food out and Houdini couldn't have made it disappear faster. On the second day Betsy showed me, in a book about the breed, that this was a behavior Rhodies engaged in and it couldn't be changed. I told her to burn the book; the writer didn't know what he was talking about. Proof was to come sooner than either of us expected.

That afternoon Mack had a vet appointment and Betsy was proud to show off his new self-control. I don't know what that dog had been doing on his previous visits, considering he couldn't have had but two or three, but by the looks of trepidation on the front office girl's face, it must have been quite a show. She observed us entering and then did a very surprised double-take as Mack sat quietly and waited his turn.

Over the next few minutes she repeatedly slid her wary look in our direction. Soon she was whispering to another girl and both of them had the look of bomb squad members in the uncomfortable position of only a few seconds remaining on the clock. As Mack was called into the exam room a sigh of relief was heard behind us. I glanced back at the receptionist and saw her drop her head to her arms. I followed Betsy into the small room and was just in time to see the vet stiffen and paste a wooden smile on his face.

I caught Mack's attention and clearly communicated that I didn't care what had been allowed in the past, it was good manners or he and I would need to talk. He exuded pained innocence, artfully intertwined with overtones of injured surprise, that I would even consider he might be anything other than a perfect gentleman... well...maybe a tad effusive with bonhomie, but still and all, a gentleman. You've got to be kidding, my look said and Mack had the good sense to look abashed at his feeble attempt to snow me.

I turned my attention to the vet, a man old enough to have a good supply of experience, and watched curiously as he engaged Betsy in a conversation, all the while surreptitiously inching his way carefully in Mack's direction. It was subtle, covert and spoke volumes about his experience with the young dog.

Mack saw his next victim approaching and I could tell his control was slipping. I could see the headlines, "Local Vet Mauled by Effusive Greeting by Dog." I cleared my throat and Mack sent me a look of disappointment. He'd planned a very special performance for this man, that much was clear, but at my reminder, he settled himself back down and with only one loss of control, a couple of quick laps of the tongue on the vet's face, he behaved almost perfectly.

It's not often I get to see a true double-take, but this vet gave a beautiful, textbook example as he knelt to listen to Mack's heart. He and Mack connected; surprise, relief and pleasure just leaked from the man. Mack swelled with pride and looked askance at me. I nodded my head slightly in acknowledgement of his achievement.

At the end of the visit the vet laid an affectionate hand on the large pup's head and spoke with great sincerity, "Good boy, Mack. I'll see you next time." It was Mack's turn to look surprised. I was pleased.

The plan for the evening was to grill out on the deck, and the three of us headed for the grocery store. Betsy stood at the meat counter and ordered filet mignons that looked wonderful, but were the base cost of a top breeding heifer back home. I tried to hide my surprise as it dawned on me just how out-of-touch I was with retail meat prices.

I raised lamb, so no purchase there, it was always available. When my dogs and

I helped a local move cattle, or I trained a dog, if the person raised beef I'd often just trade out for some meat. So, when confronted with three small pieces of mignon that cost, roughly, the same as my combined monthly land and cell phone bill, I almost keeled over. It was obvious I needed to get out more.

It was late in the afternoon when we reached the house and Betsy and I took a much needed break from training, sipped some wine and talked about nothing. Mack was allowed to play on the front lawn, while Bailey lay in the shade of the overhanging branches of a bush.

While the dogs amused themselves we moved inside to make a salad and side dishes to accompany the main course, which Jim had taken out to the side-board of the grill. To this day I'm still not certain exactly what happened, whether Jim turned his back, moved away from the grill to get something or simply was on his cell phone, but the next thing I heard was an aggrieved bellow from the front of the house.

"He's taken dinner – he's got the meat!" Jim slammed into the house with his hands in the air in a gesture of frustrated resignation.

Betsy let out a groan and stood frozen at the sink. In that instant I dropped everything, dashed around the work island, dodged a couple of dining room chairs and hit the front door at a dead run. Bursting out onto the deck I saw Mack in the process of moving away from the grill with a piece of meat clamped in his mouth. My luck, Mack's error. He hadn't gulped the food down, but was making off with it to a place where he could savor his ill-gotten booty in relative comfort and quiet. He was oblivious to everything but the savory treat that he intended to enjoy uninterrupted.

Taking two steps across the porch I grabbed Mack's collar and propelled him up against the deck railing. Shock froze the young dog in place. Rudely prying his jaws open, I retrieved the medallion of costly meat. Eyeing it quickly, I slapped it into Jim's hand and reached back into the now horrified dog's mouth and snaked my fingers into the back of his throat to save the small portion he'd managed to chew off. Whipping it out I gave it, too, to the stunned Jim.

It was a tableau. Jim stood half-way to the door with his palm up, his hand full of what had once been dinner. Betsy was half in and half out of the door watching the scene with wide-eyed surprise. Mack was sitting with a stunned look, not daring to move and not sure what had just happened. Here he'd been, planning on enjoying a nice piece of quality beef when, out of the blue, an avenging fury had swept down, growling a menacing, death-promising "aahht," while rudely shoving a hand down his gullet to retrieve his bounty. This just simply didn't happen in his world.

"It's in good shape, he only slobbered on it. Wash it off, I'll eat it."

Jim, almost as surprised as Mack, shook his head, "No, we have other cuts, I'll just get one." He began to laugh and headed inside.

"That's what he does when we leave food out on the counter." Betsy now stood beside me somewhat bewildered.

"Not around me, he doesn't. That was MY dinner and he's going to learn what happens when he takes my food."

Pushing Mack off the deck I began to "go Amish." He was shunned. He was outside our circle. He was not allowed to be within fifteen feet of the deck. I raised my arm like an avenging God banishing the sinner to purgatory, gave a growl and made it abundantly clear Mack was persona non grata because of the theft.

The young Rhodie was horrified and sped out onto the lawn. He turned to look back and I raised my arm once more and took a step toward him. He slunk away until he was some twenty feet from us and then turned and sat watching me. His eyebrows were wrinkled in grave concern. His body was tense. His eyes never left me as I turned and mounted the steps.

"I need to eat out here on the deck, is

that OK?"

"How long does he have to stay out there?" Betsy nodded in agreement and began to transfer plates in her hand to the outside table. "Until I'm certain he's learned his lesson."

We dined to a beautiful sunset and sat back relaxing as a mild breeze played around us. Out on the lawn Mack grew more uncomfortable with his isolation and at one point stood and took a few tentative steps towards us in hopes of forgiveness. I pushed my chair back and before I'd even reached a full stand, the pup had quickly resumed his original position.

John had joined us and questioned me at length about my teaching methods and then gave me a long discourse on his dog back home. We talked about the best way to handle the problems he was experiencing and he promised he'd put what he'd learned to the test the minute he reached home. He was leaving late that night and was anxious to try it out.

Bailey was enjoying the show. He had watched from the onset with nothing less than a 'nah-nah-nah' demeanor and made a great display of wandering the yard at will and returning to the deck where he was petted and talked to. Still, each time he made his way out onto the grass, he communicated clearly that Mack had better not believe him to be an ally. He, too, shunned the young dog and understood with ease what I was teaching the humans. The sun slipped down and in the gloaming I watched as Mack became visibly nervous. He repeatedly, and with great worry, looked back over his shoulder and out into the endless expanse of mesquite and arid country. There were bad things out there. They were written about in novels by Stephen King. They could come out of the dark and get you. Mack caught my eye and his growing alarm was palpable. I felt it was time to ease up a little.

We cleaned up the table and out of the corner of my eye I watched Mack become extremely concerned. He began to pace back and forth on the line of demarcation I had drawn. It was clear from his behavior and the look in his eyes he knew how badly he'd erred. It was also clear he knew he was at risk, being alone in the dark was not comfortable; he was good and truly worried. I was satisfied.

Jim and John were inside and Betsy and I were still on the porch. I rose and Mack came to attention. Opening the door and hitting the light I let Bailey enter the house. Betsy followed the old Lab and stood just inside and watched. With my hand on the door handle I stopped and looked at Mack. He was standing taut and hopeful, being out in the dark on the edge of the plains was leaving him vulnerable and he didn't like it one little bit.

With a slight nod in his direction I eased up on the emotional force field I'd established and the relief from Mack hit me like a wave. His face registered relief and joy and he fairly shouted, "Thank God, I'm forgiven!" He bounded toward me and I snapped to face him full on. He came to a screeching halt half-way to the porch.

"What's going on?" Betsy's voice floated on the gathering night.

"Mack thinks it's all over and we've forgiven him. He's wrong. He needs to learn that he's back with the group, but he's not IN the group – yet."

Keeping my gaze stern and fixed upon him I clearly communicated, without a word, that Mack could join us, but he was on probation. How he behaved would determine if we accepted him back into the group. He got the message and came carefully up the steps with no bounding, puppy enthusiasm or silly antics. He walked cautiously into the house and made his way to his bed and lay down without bothering Bailey. He didn't move.

"Well, that's a difference." Jim went into his office to finish off some work with an amused grin in our direction and a nod of his head toward the silent dog. Betsy and I talked companionably for a while longer and then decided to turn in.

"What are you going to do with him?"

"Put him in his crate. He needs to think about things." I called to the now sleeping Mack and his eyes flew open. "Mack, come." Slowly he rose to his feet and made his way to me. I opened his crate door and indicated that he should enter. Slipping by me he pushed himself to the extreme rear of his haven and curled up. I closed the door without having said a word. I caught Betsy's concern.

"Mack did something no dog should ever do – he took food from the leader. He needed to learn how egregious that behavior was. We never touched him, never had to strike him, never raised our voices, never practiced or rewarded his NOT doing it and never used a choke chain. But, he knows that he came close to losing his place in this group because his actions were so bad. The pack would have done the same thing under the same circumstances. It's all psychological and emotional. He won't do it again - if you communicate clearly that you won't stand for it either." We turned off the light and headed off to bed.

Even though I was exhausted and had been working Mack for the entire day, I still had emails and phone calls to make in order to catch up on work. It was late when I finally dropped into bed and it was later than usual when I arose the next morning.

I met up with Betsy coming down the hall and with only a nod of our heads we silently groped toward the kitchen and the life-giving coffee. With cups in hand we let the dogs out and settled ourselves deep into the deck chairs. Nothing much was said until we'd both reached our second cups.

"This is it, the last day I have with Mack, and I want to make certain he has a good, solid 'come' on him."

"It would be nice," Betsy didn't sound as if she believed it possible. "I can't catch him, he won't listen...I just don't know."

"He'll be fine, we've just spent two days teaching him who's boss. He'll listen."

At that exact moment Mack's head flew up and his body went rigid. Facing the long drive toward the gate, he held his position for two seconds and burst into action. He was off at a dead run, covering almost half a mile in an amazingly short time before his owner could reach her feet. I was impressed in spite of myself. I could see the lineage of this dog racing the plains of Africa, his speed, physical prowess and intelligence having been passed through the generations to this moment. It was living beauty that I couldn't help but admire, even if it was going in the wrong direction.

"Mack!" Betsy's strained voice mirrored her concern.

"Betsy, don't call like that, you sound worried and he won't respond." I let out a hard, high whistle. Mack spun instantly and without hesitation and headed back in our direction without a break in speed. Heading for me like a runaway freight train I had a moment's concern that he'd forget to stop and barrel into me.

"Steady...." Mack slowed, came to a stop in front of me and dropped to a sit. The young pup was barely winded as I reached down and, for the first time since I'd arrived, I petted him with true admiration and affection said, "Good come, Mack. That's what I wanted." He swelled with pride and openly basked in my pleasure.

"There's your come. It's solid now. You won't have to worry."

For the remainder of the day Betsy, Mack and I practiced and worked on little behavioral things, the kind of things that made life easier for all. At random moments while Mack was at play, out running, or merely out behind the house, I'd whistle him up and he'd appear instantly. Each time Mack was confronted with a behavioral-obedience expectation and met it correctly, Betsy relaxed a tad more and her trust in the big dog grew.

I liked this dog. Big, physically powerful, intelligent and pushy, with an incredible reserve of mental strength, Mack had an immense amount of potential. If he reached it, it would be because his owners worked hard at being consistent in their expectations.

We two women spent that last evening on the porch with the dogs stretched out in slumber. Our talk was about families, grandchildren and everything except dogs. In the far reaches of the house the phone rang and Betsy excused herself. I took my cue from the dogs and remained unmoving. The sun held low over the horizon and its warmth made the evening air a pleasant place in which to sit. Betsy's voice was a musical backdrop to the glory of the sunset.

Suddenly both dogs raised their heads and looked toward the door as Betsy, laughing hard, came out onto the deck. Handing the phone to me she said, "Here, it's John, he wants to talk to you."

"Hey, how are you?"

"It worked. By God, it worked." John's enthusiasm knew no bounds. "I got home from the airport and the silly dog was bouncing around, jumping on everyone and I let loose with an "aahht," and it worked. My wife thinks I'm nuts, but the dog actually sat down and stopped being the idiot we all know and love. This is great – you'll have to come out here and do a clinic."

"That's great. I'd love to."

Handing the phone back to Betsy I looked down at Bailey and smiled. The old

Lab seemed to share my amusement and thumped his tail twice on the wooden planks before he dropped his head back down with a huge sigh. I agreed and let my own head fall back to rest on the chair and went back to sipping wine with contentment.

Early the next morning we made the drive to the airport and I thanked Betsy and hugged Mack. I really would miss him. It was a rare thing when I wished I could take a dog home with me, yet that's how I felt as I made my good-byes to the affectionate pup. I could see so much in Mack that I knew could be brought out if he was guided correctly. His life would be wonderful and all that met him would admire him. I hoped it would come true for him.

Betsy and I spoke only a few times after I reached home. About a year or so later Tom, his wife, Janet, and I were talking and the subject of Mack came up as the two of them had recently been visiting at Betsy's and Jim's. They described Mack as having grown into a physically gorgeous dog with a wonderful, fun temperament, but still ruling the roost as Betsy had slacked off on insisting on good behavior and he had re-established himself as controller of his environment.

Tom, however, was quick to say that Mack only got the upper-hand with people he could manipulate. In the case of Janet and Tom, Mack understood immediately that they were not willing to cede the ground and be pushed around and so he followed their rules, the rules I'd spent three days teaching him.

I was torn. Part of me was extremely proud and pleased to hear the wonderful pup had matured into a magnificent dog that still remembered the lessons I had taught him and could behave well with those that expected the best of him. The other part, however, was saddened to hear that Mack was not expected to behave as a rule and so, very few people would see the best he had to offer. It was especially difficult as I had grown to love that dog in the incredibly short time we'd been together.

In my mind's eye I hold the vision that was the promise of power as the burnt-gold, savanna grass-colored body streaked away from me down the drive in pursuit of a rabbit. The agile, willing turn at my whistle and the joy radiating from the young dog as he flew back to me and settled at my feet. I remember Mack's content, intelligent eyes searching mine for a clue as to what next I desired, and what it was that would make me happy. His gaze shone with a willingness to follow my lead and his outright delight to learn that coming when called pleased me and I shared that delight and my affection with him readily. I transfered all that to the dog I know he could, and should, be. That's what I will always remember about that very special dog, because of the love and hopes I came to have for him.

Mack, Rhodesian ridgeback, age 3+ months

Like so many dogs, Mack was not bad, merely a dog.

Often when smart, mentally and physically powerful dogs enter the human house, they take over. Not as a challenge to the human, but because they are confident, quick in their ability to see opportunities, graced with the physical prowess to force control or change upon their environment, and supremely self-confident.

It's the confidence that quite frequently causes the most amount of trouble, as the dog simply sees what he would like to have, or thinks should happen and makes it reality. He never even considers the humans in the equation as they have failed, or been remiss, in laying down the rules and have been inconsistent in their expectations of behavior and obedience.

Since most humans are much slower at learning to read their dog than the dog is at learning to read their human, the owners trail behind in the wake of misbehavior and rarely find the opportunity to re-establish that they're in charge. The human is always reactive, not pro-active. Frequently the follower, rarely the leader. Often nagging, rarely the commanding.

In the few instances that the owner actually gets ahead of the dog and manages to stop the behavior at the thinking point, the dog, being the intelligent, opportunistic creature it is, changes tactics and tries something new in order to achieve its goal. This often works.

Mack was one such dog. He could adjust his tactics and behavior to the individual, adapting and overcoming the person's resistance. He was successful, in part, because the humans only dealt with him in human terms. If, for instance, they wished to stop him from biting arms, they would grab him. This played to his strength and allowed him to win the resulting wrestling match. He had teeth, agility, four feet on the floor and speed, not to mention leverage. He won. He also enjoyed the challenge and it was a game to him.

If he stole food, the human scolded him. He might have been somewhat abashed or appalled that his behavior elicited that specific response from his owner, but as nothing truly happened to endanger his standing in the group, psychologically or physically, the human display was soon dismissed as ineffectual and of no consequence. There was really no downside for Mack when he was dealt with in human terms.

When, however, Mack was dealt with in the manner that dogs deal with each other and he met an implacable force that could read him well enough to stop the thought before it became action by applying the correct amount of psychological pressure, as well as blocking the physical action, he behaved as any dog would and willingly gave respect to the leader. He was then anxious to please the more competent, smarter, more psychologically adept individual on a consistent and ongoing basis, not hit or miss. He didn't need to be trained in WHAT to do; he learned what was NOT acceptable and stopped doing it. That simple. It is another case which proves "Behavior begets obedience, obedience does NOT beget behavior."

He would never be an easy-going dog like his counterpart, Bailey, because Mack's temperament was not the same. His curiosity, need for physical and mental challenge, self-confidence, and natural leadership bent precluded his being a laid-back, take-it-or-leave-it kind of dog, But, he would be a well-mannered, willing dog. It simply meant his owners would need to be more aware, more consistent, more on top of his behavior and have higher expectations from him, because he tended to push without deliberate intent or regard for those around him.

Mack needed people who clearly defined what was acceptable, held him to the highest standards in order to drain physical and mental energy, never used excuses as to why he didn't meet those standards, and didn't allow him to deviate from what they set as behavioral rules until such time as Mack had made good behavior a habit.

Without all of these things Mack just behaved as any dog would and constantly tested, challenged and experimented with his world to learn exactly what its limits were as they applied to him. The problem with this was that Mack's world and how he behaved in it inadvertently caused serious overall problems for the humans with whom he came into contact.

The goal was to teach Mack's owners how to read him; how to block his physical actions without being too physical and allowing him to turn it into a wrestling match; how to communicate commands which would be followed without creating a challenge scenario; and how to put this entire package together in order for Mack to respect them as leaders of his world.

Questions & Answers

Q: Our two-year old Golden gets very excited when people come to visit. We have to put her in a room or she jumps all over them and tears through the house. This year it's my turn to host our large family

Christmas dinner and I need to know how
I can control Jessie. Should I put her in a
boarding kennel?

A: I wish I were willing to give a short, pat
answer as so many trainers/behaviorists
offer. I just can't. I'm sure many of you
would be happier if I did. The truth, however, is that unless you see and understand
the many sides to this, and other questions,
you won't be capable of altering your behavior and/or expectations, nor the behavior of your dog. You will then, when the pat
answer doesn't achieve consistent and positive results, feel that you have somehow
failed as an owner or your dog has failed.
Neither is true. We cannot alter or improve
that which we don't understand. It is un-
realistic to expect you to change your dog's
behavior if you don't understand your com-
plicity and responsibility in condoning or
encouraging unwanted actions from your
dog, or your own behavior which elicits incorrect responses from your dog.

From the human standpoint, ken-
neling Jessie would be the easiest solution.
But, it is a band-aid not a cure for the problem. Jessie will have been removed from
the situation and have learned nothing at
all about how to greet people. So, the problem will continue to exist.

Many facets are in play in this problem. First, long ago and far away, Jessie

was out of control when people came to the house and the behavior was excused by claiming she was a pup and excited to see the new person. As she grew, and the problem grew exponentially, she was probably put outside before guests arrived or isolated as soon as her behavior began. She was not instructed as to how to appropriately behave before she ever even greeted visitors.

Second, when she exhibited hyperactive behavior she, in all probability, received a scolding or was held onto. The pleading tone or touching that normally accompanies a dog which greets in this manner only serves to lead the dog to believe their actions are acceptable. A pleading tone by a human is often interpreted by the dog as growing excitement on your part over the approach or arrival of the new person and the dog will take its behavioral cue from you. A frustrated tone tells the dog you have no power. Grabbing the dog in order to stop the jumping locks in the notion that hyper-active greeting is condoned, because amongst themselves, dogs have physical interaction when a specific behavior needs to be remembered.

Third, it is my guess that Jessie probably greets you each day when you return to the house in the same manner and it's interpreted as joy in your arrival home and it is now a long-established pattern.

Fourth, and finally, the visitors idiotically greeted the cute puppy with high-pitched tones and increased energy and thus completed the circle of misbehavior by demonstrating to the pup that this was the ritual form of greeting by humans and dogs. While the first three actions we can concentrate on and alter, the fourth—the visitor's behavior—we can only anticipate and/or block for the sake of our dog.

You have a couple of weeks before the holiday dinner and, with consistent behavioral correction, should be able to get Jessie vastly improved, if not under control. Everyone in the house will need to insist that she follow the rules. Once again—go back to square one: make her learn to sit, calm down and stay in one place until you release her.

Dogs, when unsure, fall back on the first thing they were taught. When Jessie greets a person, she falls back on the learned wrong behavior. Her greeting is an annoyance, not a positive experience for both her and the people she meets. They do not appreciate her greeting manners and convey this to her via their attitude—something dogs can read very easily. Jessie then tries harder; she becomes more out-of-control in an attempt to greet the way she believes is correct. The vicious cycle has now begun.

If, however, Jessie is taught to go lie down out of the way when people come to the house, or to sit quietly if met on the street, if she comes to understand she is not to initiate the meeting, but wait until she is signaled to greet, she will have been given time to calm down so that her approach is polite. The reception from the greeted human will be positive, thereby positively reinforcing in her mind that she has behaved well according to pack standards.

Just watch the interplay when an out-of-control dog greets a person. The greeted human moves backward (rejection), makes a face (negative emotion) and keeps his distance (dislike/shunning). The dog tries harder, the owner now becomes embarrassed (negative emotion), grabs or pulls on the dog and begins to tell it to 'stop' (frustration, lack of clear leadership, and no command/guidance for behavior). This is a negative experience all the way around for the dog. It knows the humans are not happy, it's not allowed to be social, and it's then isolated in a myriad of subtle ways and receives nothing but negative response. The dog will only try harder to do what it believes is correct in the way of greeting at the next opportunity and everything will continue to worsen.

On the other hand, when a dog is polite and waits across a room, it allows the visitor time to enter, talk to the owner, get settled and calm. (This is important as many visitors are excited to see us, especially at the holidays, and their emotions are communicated to the dog which also gets excited by virtue of the contact. By teaching your dog to sit, wait and be calm, you block an emotional jolt, making it easier for him to maintain good behavior.) When the dog finally is called to greet he approaches at a walk, quietly, and the visitor pets him, tells him calmly and with pleased sincerity he's a good dog, smiles, rests his hand on the head or continues a quiet petting motion (positive feedback to the dog for its behavior). The owner sits calmly, feeling pleased that his dog is liked (more positive feedback). The dog is then told to sit or go lie down, but allowed to remain in the company of the humans (positive pack interaction as well as satisfying curiosity and a sense of inclusion). The same holds true if the dog sits when the greeting takes place on the street.

Now, sometimes even the best dogs are faced with, and overwhelmed by, "The Invasion of the Psychotic Alien Children," the high-pitched, frantic "Aunt Mabel's Cutsey-Wootsey Dog Syndrome" or the "We Are Highly Competitive, Loud, Excited Game Players Malaise." It is at these times you'd best have a crate or quiet room handy and let the dog retire in safety. This is where you, as owner, must block human behavior which makes it almost dangerous for your dog.

Enough continued stress on the dog and it will do what it must to alleviate it—usually nip or become hyper in its attempt to join in. It is NOT a failure on the part of your dog; it is the detrimental emotional bludgeoning heaped on for an extended time by unaware humans. Even the best dog has its limits and it's our responsibility to ensure they're not pushed beyond them.

Start with Jessie right now. Teach her to calm down when you return home. Don't touch or pet her until she is totally calm and don't confuse anticipatory sitting with calm behavior. They are NOT the same thing. Insist she stay on a down across the room while you eat. Command her to go lie down in a designated spot when a visitor enters. By doing all this daily, consistently, she will understand what is expected of her when your family descends on your house.

If she begins to lose her composure on that all-important day, put her in a crate; give her time to collect herself. When you release her, send her to her spot and allow her time to calm down there, too, before including her in the group. She will amaze you and your guests. And, even if she's not perfect, try to see how far she's come in such a short time and how hard she's trying to behave correctly for you.

Reward her by including her as much as possible within the limits of her new abilities. It will make for a merrier Christmas for all.

Chapter 7

Terrorist Cell

THUMP!

I winced, my face scrunched into a grimace of pain each time I heard the heavy thud. I flinched again as the next resounding dull whomp reached my ears.

In the background I could make out the muted barking. High, static yipping accompanied by contrapuntal bass woofs, which entered into the rhythm at irregular intervals, was clearly audible even from this distance of almost twenty feet.

THUMP!

I was developing a tic under my left eye...I was sure of it.

I followed the main melody of the frantic dogs, two short barks, a long one bordering on a howl, and then a glissando bark which began on a high note and slid to the bottom register, all interwoven around the staccato yips.

I found myself holding my breath as I thought, "Right about now"...and was duly rewarded with a fingernails-on-the-blackboard sound. I hunched my shoulders and squeezed my eyes closed.

This was torture. I couldn't ignore it and I couldn't do anything about it; moving farther away wasn't going to make it any easier. I turned from where I was sitting on a tree-shaded rock and focused on this place I'd traveled almost three days to reach.

A large cedar house, of clearly modern design, with an inviting covered patio and comfortable-looking chairs held my attention. I yearned to sit on something more forgiving than the rock, but I had tried that and the din from the house's interior was overwhelming.

THUMP!

My eyes rose to the expanse of sliding glass door through which could be seen a strange array of dogs. By my count, which I was pretty sure was inaccurate because of the milling bodies, there were at least five dogs of various sizes and breed.

Beginning at about two feet and

peaking at four feet from the ground was an opaque smear which resembled spikes on a heart monitor and ran the width of both doors. The smear was enhanced by smudges artistically dotting either side of it and would have been the envy of Picasso, were he alive to see it.

Suddenly, a streaking body caught my attention. A Parson Jack Russell shot off like a bullet, made a racing lap around the family room, picking up speed as he went until he gained enough momentum to leap onto the back of the sofa and launch from there to the patio doors. THUMP! Hitting the wall of glass with all four feet he then dropped like a stone to the ground and disappeared amid the churning mass of bodies.

It took the Russell about ten seconds to disentangle himself from the pack and, with diabolical joy, head off for another lap.

There was a pattern to all of this which I began to pick up as I sat and watched. Every third lap of the Russell was accompanied by the inverted "v" smear of a nose across the door. After one back-and-forth traverse, this dog, a Welsh terrier, threw his head back and gave a surprisingly deep bark. Just one.

Interspersed was the high-pitched scritch of nails sliding down the glass as a Plummer terrier mix scrabbled at the door.

Sitting Buddha-like in the exact middle of all of this was a Boston terrier. Every so often he licked his lips, took a deep breath, threw his head back and, in totally non-Boston fashion, made a valiant attempt to howl. It left much to be desired. I like terriers. But this woman was either on a mission from God, or paying penance for terrible sins to own this many, varied terriers. The word "masochistic" floated across my mind.

I had arrived the evening before, having driven almost straight through from my home in Montana to Ohio in response to an emergency request for help, and after checking into a nice room, had slept like the dead. The arrangement was to meet Kelly at eight, but she had warned me she might run late as she needed to drop her youngest child at school. So it was I sat on a rock in her yard and was treated to a front-row seat of her dogs and their behavior.

There was a sudden halt to all activity and noise from within the house and then, in an instant, the dogs turned as one and ran pell-mell across the family room and into the kitchen barking and jostling each other. I half-rose from my seat as I watched one of the dogs bump an end table and send a very expensive lamp swaying. It was futile, I knew I couldn't save it: still, I sprang to my feet and stood poised to catch it until it had ceased its rocking and resumed an undisturbed, upright position. I let out a sigh of relief.

The dogs were returning, I could tell by the increased sound. Struggling to make her way through the churning horde at her feet, I observed a small woman who couldn't have been much taller than five-feet and who was dressed neatly in slacks and polo shirt and had a glorious head of Irish-red hair.

She repeatedly pushed away the nose of the Welsh terrier, which seemed to leap very close to her height in its efforts to lick her face. Alternately, she gave a leg-jerk to dislodge the Plummer which had attached itself to her knee. The Boston, intent on getting his share of affection, made a continuous figure eight around her ankles, snuffling and drooling on her pant legs. The Russell had adroitly managed to use the kitchen chairs to reach the counter top on which he now ran back and forth. Without breaking stride, Kelly reached over, scooped him up and deposited him on the floor. He shot off on another speed lap.

I suddenly caught a glimpse of a white body I hadn't seen before. Following the rioting mob was a seemingly sedate, well-mannered Westie. He refused to be coerced into the chaos of the pack and simply trailed calmly behind, as if waiting for acknowledgement. My eyebrows rose.

Then I saw it; as the Welsh terrier descended from a jump, the Westie struck with
amazing speed, nipped the larger dog hard
enough it send it back-peddling to the wall
and moved one place closer to its owner.
It was a great tactical move by the
sturdy dog. Keep calm, watch for opportunities, strike like lightening and my owner
will be oblivious of my terrorist capabilities.
The other dogs, however, were very aware of
the Westie's intent and began to focus more
on him. Even the larger dogs, the Welsh
and Plummer, gave way in the face of the
West Highland terrier's silent determination, and soon he was right where he had
intended to be all the time, next to Kelly.

"Hi," Kelly sang out as she opened
the nose-smeared glass door.

I stood as the entire group pushed
their way as one through the door and ran,
tumbled and body-slammed their way to
greet me.

"Hi." I looked down with an evil glare
at the pack of dogs as they all rudely began
to investigate me and demand my attention.

Harry, the Welsh terrier, jumped up,
his front paws solidly hitting my mid-sec-
tion, knocking the breath out of me and
forcing me to brace myself in order not to
fall over backwards from his enthusiastic
assault.

Misty, the Plummer mix, was behind

me with her nose planted firmly in the seat of my pants, breathing in and out deeply, and every so often letting loose a large, wet sneeze. I didn't even want to think about it.

The cuff of my left pant leg was firmly grasped by Beans, the Boston, who was giving it all he had as he tried valiantly to pull me off balance.

Jumping unceasingly as high as he could, much in the manner of a psychotic kangaroo was, Manfred, the Jack Russell. If nothing else it was an impressive display of agility and strength as the small dog reached heights I hadn't thought possible without the aid of a trampoline. At the apex of each leap he let out a breathless yip that could have shattered glass.

And last, but far from least, a covert operation was being put into action by Jock, the Westie, who had quietly walked up, sniffed my pants and was now urinating copiously, intent on drenching leg, sock and tennis shoe. I pulled my foot out of the way hastily, but the damage had been done.

I felt the tic under my eye take up the beat again.

"Jock, no!" Kelly grabbed his collar and pulled the Westie back away from my leg as he continued making his mark. "Bad boy! I'm so sorry. Can I offer you something to drink?" With one hand still holding Jock, Kelly used her free hand to attempt to push away the other dogs. It was an exercise in futility as the second she managed to stop one dog, another took its place. I was in the canine wing of Bedlam and the inmates were running the asylum. As she slogged her way to the kitchen to fulfill my request for a cup of coffee, the dogs following in her wake, I sank gratefully into a chair on the patio. I watched her return as she traversed the family room, cup in hand, without spilling a drop. No mean feat considering the riotous mob of dogs surrounding her.

She cleared Beans from the chair across from me only to have it instantly occupied by Manfred. Pushing him off she began to sit and had to, once again, remove Beans. Kelly picked the Boston up and deposited him on the floor and I watched Manfred immediately take up the vacated position. After four attempts to clear a spot to sit, Kelly gave up and perched precariously on the edge of the cushioned seat and let the dogs have their way behind her.

"Thank you for coming. They love company and can get a little excited." Kelly, without even batting an eyelash, reached over and grabbed Manfred who was now walking all over the patio table, and placed him on the ground. He jumped back into the chair and up on the table again nosing my coffee, licking Kelly's face and pacing back and forth between the two of us.

Several times she removed the offending Manfred without saying a word. Each time the Russell returned to the table top. Finally Kelly ignored him and let him stay perched in his aerie.

I could not believe this. Kelly didn't seem in the least perturbed by the insanity surrounding her. It was a testimony to just what a human could adapt to and survive. I knew I would have committed hari kari long ago.

"I have a problem."

This was good. Admitting you have a problem with your dog is the first step in recovery. I waited without a word.

"I called you because Ben, my husband, is out of town for another two weeks on business. He left a week ago. A few days ago the dogs caused a small problem and I'd like to ensure it doesn't happen again. Casey, my friend, used you and swears you can do wonders. I'd like to get some training for them before Ben returns – and without him knowing."

I was totally lost and my face must have reflected that. Kelly stood, "Maybe you'd better see it."

I rose and followed her across the lawn as the dogs sped hither and yon, dashing to us and then away to the farthest reaches of the yard, bringing toys, body-checking each other and even knocking over a wooden planter full of mums. Kelly continued as if nothing were amiss.

Reaching for the knob of the garage door, she turned, "I had Harry and Jock with me and don't know which one did this, but I need to get it fixed before Ben returns and I need to make certain the boys don't do this again."

We entered a large, tidy, three-car garage and the only vehicle in it was parked in shadow at the far end. Kelly flipped the switch and a shaft of light as if from heaven fell directly on the gleaming car - a gorgeous metallic, dove-gray Mercedes E63 AMG Wagon. I didn't know a thing about cars, but it was easy to see the quality and realize the price for this car was the annual budget of a small country. It was breathtaking and its beauty was apparent in its every line.

She moved across the garage to stand by the car and I followed. "This is why I called you."

"What a wonderful car." I'm sure I sounded a tad envious.

"Yes, it is, I love it. The night before he left we celebrated my birthday and Ben gave it to me as a present." I made a mental note to have a serious talk with my family before my next birthday. I was obviously doing something very wrong.

"It goes in the shop tomorrow. It has

to," Kelly was emphatic.

"I was only in the grocery store maybe thirty minutes." She opened the car doors. "I don't think Ben would be happy if he saw this." There was just the slightest hint of worry to her voice.

"Oh....my...God!" I was horror struck and my breath rushed out of me.

Not be happy? Not be HAPPY?? The car must have cost upwards of $80,000 and Ben would not be happy? No, no, no. If I were Ben I'd go on a five-state killing spree. I'd sell the dogs to a culture that considered them a delicacy. I'd hang myself from the rafters. Not be happy? That was an understatement.

I stood rooted to the spot and stared into the interior of the car. It was a soft charcoal gray color, with a leather interior that begged to be touched. Or, at least, it HAD begged to be touched.

Now it resembled something which had barely survived a full-blown Viking raid.

The entire middle section was awash in reams of fluff. Stuffing was scattered all over and covered the carpeted floor. The leather was almost black and chewed to a pulp, hanging in stringy masses from the back and seat. The seatbelts were reduced to frayed and discolored webbing, lying bedraggled in tangles amidst the carnage.

The driver and passenger headrests

were mere shadows of their former selves. Chewed to the frame in some places, punctured in a thousand more.

The console between the front seats was missing. Gone—reduced to confetti-like pieces on the seats and floor.

The steering wheel and emergency brake handle bore the marks of determined teeth. A forensic pathologist would have salivated to take the dental impressions, so numerous and clear were the imprints.

The arm rest on the passenger side, along with the entire door paneling was ripped, twisted, chewed, and drooled on. The carnage stood as mute testimony to demonic possession.

As I took in the devastation, I noted that there was a metal divider between the rear cargo area and the seats. "Was that divider in place when this happened?"

"Oh, yes. But one of the dogs pulled it down."

"We need to talk."

Back on the patio Kelly began to tell me how each of the dogs had come to be a part of the family. With the exception of Jock, whom they had gotten as a pup, the others had been cast-offs the couple had adopted.

The oldest of the group was Beans, who was seven. The youngest, Misty, was three. The others ranged in age between these two. All had been through obedience class.

"You're telling me that every dog here has completed obedience?" I was shocked. But, then again, I wasn't.

"Oh, yes, and some, like Misty, more than once." Kelly seemed embarrassed.

"Then why aren't they being obedient?" I queried.

"They all do fine in class. They even mind if they're on a leash, alone, with me. But, as a group, we can't control them."

"Have you asked a trainer for help?"

"Yes," Kelly pushed Harry away from her ear, lifted Manfred from the table and placed him on the floor and dislodged Beans from the seat behind her so that she might lean back in the chair. "He came to the house, worked for about three hours and then told us that we needed to take them to obedience class, that we simply needed to practice obedience more."

I was unsure how to respond. I don't like to directly criticize another trainer, but I also felt this was not something I could let slide without comment. I thought, however, it was prudent to get some more information before I made any further comments.

"What forms of obedience have the dogs been through?"

"Manfred started with clicker, but failed. We then took him to a regular class, the kind with the choke chain?"

Counting on her fingers she ticked

off each remaining dog. "Harry, positive reinforcement. Misty went through the certified trainer at the local shelter. Beans went through the same two classes with Manfred. Harry was taught by a woman who shows AKC dogs."

"Why do you think you have this problem, then?"

"I really don't know. Ben and I practiced with the dogs, every day just like we were told. They seem to do alright for a while, then something goes wrong. When the group is together it's as if they've never had obedience." With a defeated look she watched the dogs playing in the yard.

"I love my dogs. The trainers have all told me that terriers can't be trusted off-leash, that they're hard to train and not dependable a lot of times. Ben is coming to the end of his tolerance with them, and the destruction of the car may be his last straw." Kelly's worried gazed turned on me, "Casey said you could fix this."

"Alright, we begin now." I issued instructions about the various dogs and Kelly and I began to work. We began with Jock, as he was clearly in charge.

For the next three hours Kelly was inundated with dog information and how to handle each dog as they were reintroduced into the group. We took a brief lunch and were hard at it for the remainder of the afternoon.

By four o'clock I could tell Kelly couldn't take in any more information and was exhausted. The dogs were tired, too. My main worry was how she would handle the next morning. We'd made great strides and I didn't want it all undone as she went about her morning routine.

"Kelly, normally I don't do this, but I was wondering if it would be okay for me to stay here tonight? That way, in the morning, I can show you how to ensure they all start the day quietly and correctly."

Her pleasure and relief were palpable and she offered to drive me to the hotel, get my things and get me settled into her guest room.

I heard the alarm go off in another room and lay in bed gathering my thoughts. Suddenly the thundering hoard could be heard racing down the hallway and a maelstrom of solid bodies crashed into the room. Harry made a flying leap and landed squarely on my stomach. The breath was knocked out of me and I uttered an ugly sounding "umph." This seemed to be the cue for the other dogs to join us. I was smothered under an avalanche of wriggling, licking, investigating bodies.

"Aaahhhtt!"

The dogs all froze in place. The dawning of understanding rose on their faces as I struggled from beneath them. Extricating myself from the bed I took a step toward the door and they all exploded, once again, into movement.

"Aahhtt!" Misty froze in place with her hind quarters on the duvet and her front feet on the floor. The others stood rooted to their spots.

"Uh-uh!" I uttered menacingly as I crossed the room and closed the door. Then I turned and shot a nasty look in the dogs' direction. Misty, still half-on and half-off the bed slowly lowered her rear end to a contorted sit position.

I began to get dressed. The dogs all watched me as I ran through the morning ablutions, but none moved. As my hand descended on the doorknob the dogs rose to their feet as one, Balanchine would have been proud.

"Ah ah," I uttered warningly. Manfred, Beans, Harry and Jock all returned to a sit, but Misty, still with her back end elevated on the bed, stood uncertainly. It was obvious she would have preferred to be completely on or completely off the bed, but was not willing to push the issue. Finally, she opted for discretion and lowered her derriere to the duvet once again.

Quietly I called the dogs to me and insisted they walk as we made our way down the hall and into the kitchen. Kelly, in her robe, was pouring coffee for us both. She turned and her mouth popped open. The "Fearsome Five," as I'd dubbed them, had all sat and were watching her silently.

Cocking my head at the group, I gave a warning look and headed over to grab the cup of coffee. Taking the cup, which was now tilted at a dangerous angle in Kelly's hand, I wandered toward the patio door. Silence reigned and not a soul had moved.

"Jock."

The Westie cocked his head at me in a ruminative and beguiling manner. He clearly conveyed his thought that this must be some sort of trick.

"Jock." I was a bit more insistent. "Come." Manfred stood with anticipation. "Manfred – aahht." I countered quietly. The Russell slowly returned to a sit.

"Jock." My tone was now warning. The Westie slowly rose to his feet, glanced at his fellow dogs, and walked carefully over to the door. He looked up at me and after a moment, sat and waited. I opened the door and let him out. He sedately wandered out into the yard and began sniffing.

"Misty." The Plummer immediately sprang to her feet.

"Misty, walk." With great effort the young terrier gathered herself into a state of control and came to me. I let her out.

Each dog in turn repeated the process until only Manfred was left. Alone in the middle of the kitchen floor, the Russell's head snapped to and fro as he looked first at Kelly then at me, tensed and waiting to be released.

"Is he going to go out?" asked Kelly, finding her voice for the first time that morning.

"Sure, when he calms down." The small dog sat poised for the dash, adrenalin coursed through the compact body, making him shake with anticipation. Every muscle was bunched for the great push-off and he was listening intently for the release word.

"Thank you for the coffee."

"Certainly." Kelly was both surprised and confused and the two emotions battled for supremacy.

For the next five minutes I made small talk with Kelly. I monitored Manfred and his behavior. At last the smart dog realized he'd not be going out and it was best to relax. Suddenly he lay down and let out a sigh.

"We'll let him hold that for a couple of minutes then he can go out." The small dog cocked his ear at the word, but didn't move.

I finished my coffee, made another cup and moved to the door. The tenseness returned to Manfred's body. Leaning against the jamb I watched both the dogs in the yard and the one in the kitchen.

"Manfred, come." He jerked to alertness, but didn't move. I called him again and he shot to me, skittering across the tile, gaining traction and speed on the rug of the family room floor and ending, finally, with a forepaw-scrabble on the glass of the sliding door.

Calmly I reached down, took hold of his collar and led him back to his spot in the kitchen. We tried again. Manfred was an incredibly bright dog and it took all of two times for him to discern the new rule. On the third try he succeeded in walking to the door, albeit tensely, sat, waited, and went outside in a controlled manner.

Once outside the door, however, he exploded and made a mad dash straight at Beans. The reaction was not what he expected. The other dogs, having gone outside quietly and independently, were not engaging in their normal mayhem. As Manfred raced to each dog, intent on inciting the glorious morning riot, they refused to respond. Soon he gave up and trotted happily around the expanse of grass doing his morning chores. He visited politely with his mates, but remained a gentleman.

"How did you do that?" Kelly's voice mirrored her stunned demeanor.

"We removed Jock as pack leader and stopped Manfred from acting as an emotional cattle-prod to the group."

When the time came to bring the dogs back in the house I had Kelly reverse the entire scenario. She struggled to make them sit, but with some guidance she succeeded, and then, individually she called them in and sent them to lie down. All the dogs followed her instructions with varying degrees of compliance. But, she was successful and her pleasure was evident to all the dogs.

I remained an extra day; Kelly and I decided that we needed the extra time to make certain both she and the dogs were on the right path.

It was still dark as I dressed and got ready to depart. Kelly and her dogs saw me to the car and I said goodbye to each of the sitting dogs.

"They're a great group, Kelly. I'll miss them."

With a last pat on the head for the dogs and a hug from Kelly, I headed out the drive and the long trip home.

A last glance in the rearview mirror showed Kelly reaching the front door, all the dogs walking beside her and then they sat, waiting calmly to enter their house.

Kelly contacted me a few times over the subsequent months with questions. None were real problems, merely how best to handle a situation.

One day I received an email from her. It was bubbling with pride. She recounted how she'd taken all five dogs to the local park, off-leash, and had unexpectedly encountered an obedience class full of rambunctious dogs.

Misty, Beans, Harry and Jock had all ignored the group, but Manfred had made a dash toward the class. Kelly called to him and he stopped in his tracks. With only a small warning to him, he returned to her group and they continued without a mishap. Her pride in her dogs knew no bounds as she heard someone say, "I want to be able to walk my dog off-leash and get her to listen like that."

Attached to Kelly's email were two photographs from Ben. The first showed the metal divider in the trashcan and on it was a large sign which read, "Thank You." The second photo was of all the dogs sitting in the back of the restored and gorgeous-as-ever Mercedes wagon.

The Pack, all terriers, various ages

This was a case of dogs establishing a pack and humans being side-lined. The dogs allowed the humans into their world and Jock was the undisputed leader of the group.

He meted out discipline and rules, owned the humans, and commanded the respect of the other dogs. The humans were included as an afterthought and were tolerated as a weak supply line of food and amusement. They were not respected and so were not accorded the good behavior which accompanies respect.

Manfred, however, was the battery. He supplied the energy which riled the group and sent them into high, octane-fueled mayhem. The others, Misty, Beans and Harry, fell somewhere in the middle as far as energy and compliance. It was necessary to dethrone Jock and install Kelly as leader. Once that was achieved, the next step was to teach Manfred to calm down. Kelly and Ben could not control the pack without these two issues being resolved.

After reasserting human leadership into the group via Kelly, the dogs' behavior altered substantially and they offered her the respect and obedience to her commands and behavioral expectations due her as leader.

When Kelly became aware and could identify Manfred's rising excitement, and not write it off as a Jack Russell trait, she was capable of insisting that he calm down. This elevated her position as leader and increased her self-confidence and control over the dogs, individually and as a pack, as well.

All of this together meant that fewer and fewer problems arose which Kelly could not handle. She needed only to indicate her expectations in the way of behavior and the dogs complied. They relaxed into an accepting, well-behaved pack under her guidance.

Questions & Answers

Q: "I have three dogs, a Labrador, a terrier mix, and a Cocker Spaniel mix, all are from the shelter or rescued. I'm in obedience class with the lab now, the other two have taken obedience. When all three are together it's out of control. They're all pretty good if they're alone with me, but I can't get them to listen at home or outside when they're together. What's going on? Why isn't it working?"

A: You are one of many owners living and functioning under these conditions.

The dogs are faced with trainers who train, but don't know dogs. Dogs are subjected to this quite a bit with humans.

More and more dogs are being rescued. This is a good thing. More and more rescued dogs are living with behavioral problems which make them, and their owners, miserable because many trainers don't know dogs.

You can't fix a problem if you don't understand how the whole of the thing works in the first place. You can merely band-aid the observable. This results in the underlying issues building up until they erupt in unexpected ways and places.

It means many dogs can't live normal lives. They may have been saved from death, but they cannot live. They are not trusted. They can't be allowed freedoms. They don't find peace of mind. They are confronted daily with their owner's fear and other people's rejection of them due to their behavior. They are not dealt with in a manner which allows them to interact and move forward to be a part of a loving life. This is the ultimate hell for a dog. It's emotionally and physically isolated, has no surcease from pressure and fear and no allies. Its body has been saved, but its mind and life are captive to a hell most humans don't even recognize.

If one concentrates on only training the body of the dog it is a long and arduous task and is rarely successful in long-term, permanent behavioral changes which are beneficial to both dog and human. The dogs, and the owners, go through hell in order to achieve obedience and often are kept in hell because the dog wasn't helped psychologically and socially.

Many owners and trainers can work with dogs for weeks and not achieve what is truly possible to achieve in a matter of hours if they only knew dogs. It is because the training is not effective that the dog is said to have "failed" obedience class. The most important thing to me is that both the dog and owner succeed and reach a place of trust, understanding and happiness together, along with good behavior which is clear and understood by the dog so as to make its life easier and better all around. Having said all that, we must dump thinking about obedience as the 'fix', especially when we're talking about dogs in a group situation. Obedience is the icing, but if there is no cake, what good is it?

First and foremost, one needs to recognize that the vast majority of dogs in adoptive situations are there due to behavioral problems. These issues were created and allowed to become substantial by owners and, probably, trainers. Some of the rescued dogs have been through obedience training, some have not. But, all have failed to have behavioral parameters set. Behavioral parameters are vastly different from obedience expectations.

An owner can only avail himself of the training options out there. Book knowledge about dogs' behavior is a long way from truly knowing about dogs. True knowledge about dogs has been derived through innate skill, living, and working with dogs. By working, I mean actual years of physical work that both dog and owner do together. Not merely showing the dog or competing with it in agility. Not training other peoples' dogs, part-time, on the weekend. I mean actually working with a group of his own dogs where personalities, temperaments, frustrations, drive, instinct, jealousy, competition, applicable skills, extrapolated skills evidenced by the thinking dog, trust, learning curves, working environment adaptations, physical freedom, wrecks and more must be dealt with on a daily basis, all the while attempting to work other animals which are involved in, and experiencing, many of these same issues, at the same time, within their group and the animals are not controlled by a leash.

I have seen people involved with a working dog and just through daily job interaction learn quite a bit about dogs in general and not even realize it. Their confidence increases. They are stronger in their control of their dog(s). They are more quickly aware of the dog which is not behaving. They are more relaxed in their relationship with their dog. This also holds true of those owners who spend almost all their time with their dog(s) and take them everywhere with them. It is also true of full-time trainers that have worked dogs for years or have a natural affinity with dogs.

Lack of confidence in themselves, and in their dog, is the first major problem owners face and is of primary importance. Without self-confidence, the dog will not trust nor follow. Without self-confidence, the owner engenders fear in the dog and within himself. Without self-confidence, the owner creates the scenario whereby what he fears most comes to reality.

Ninety-nine out of one hundred trainers never see this human problem and its importance to the basic psychological makeup of the dog, and so it is never addressed. If they cannot identify this as a major problem for both dog and owner, then how can they truly teach? They can not. Which is why obedience is rote learning for conditioned response. It is NOT truly capable of helping the dog, and owner, with the psychological, behavioral and social problems exhibited and acted out.

So, the first skill which must be mastered by an owner is self-confidence. With that he non-verbally communicates to the new, insecure, searching dog that he is leader. The dog easily recognizes the most confident member of any group (the leader in his mind) and begins to watch closely how this person handles all situations. It gives the dog a sense of peace and security once he understands that this confident individual will solve food, housing, relationship, behavioral, sexual, and hierarchical, rule making/breaking and following, and distribution of resource problems. In short, the confident person non-verbally indicates that "the buck stops here" to the dog. The dog can then relax and begin to exhibit some self-confidence of its own.

Problem One can have a complication. Should there be no defined confident leader, then the dog will step up and take on that mantle. They don't like it. They don't want it. But, since they don't perceive a leader, as dogs identify a leader, they are compelled to take on the responsibility and the problem is now behavioral, for the dog as leader will not behave in a manner which the human likes. If the dog doesn't get the response he feels due him as the leader, he'll discipline in the manner of dogs. He'll bite. He'll believe he has the right to explore at will his territory, as any good leader should, and he will ignore commands. He will take first portion of any food which is in his vicinity as any dog leader would. He will possess the terrain, as it is his right as leader to choose where, when and how he wishes to relax and sleep and the rest of us should make do. He will expect all others in his group to follow him and his lead. He will defend his right to be leader. It is in his psychological and genetic makeup to do this. This, then, is when he's taken to obedience class and it actually becomes, in the dog's mind, a challenge by the owner for leadership. This is not something the dog will easily capitulate on once he has taken on the role. Usually, the dog and owner fail the class. Or, at best, the outcome is erratic consistency in following commands.

The confidence portion as conveyed by the leader, if there is any, usually takes about three to five weeks to become firmly acknowledged by the dog and love has no place in his assessment at this time other than to suggest weakness in the human as perceived by the dog. The dog now begins to test the boundaries it has witnessed to determine if and how they apply to him. This natural process is in the best interest of the dog. He must be sure that the leader can do what is advertised. The testing also allows the dog to determine if his jostling will move his position in the pack closer to the leader.

Thus begins Problem Two. In his testing, the dog willfully pushes the limits. He tests others in the pack to see if they will crumple in the face of his determination. This is also testing the leader--can he/will he stop me? Is my bid for upward mobility acceptable? It won't matter if the "others" in the pack are children, roommates, spouses, dogs or cats. The natural desire of the dog will be to elevate himself, physically and socially, above the rest. This will allow him greater freedoms, more food, and to become closer to the established leader with all its perks. It will also allow him to learn greater leadership skills and thus be in a position to step into the role of, or challenge, the pack leader in the future.

This means an owner must ensure that ALL dogs in their group understand that A) the owner is leader; B) all humans are above dogs in the pack; and C) there is only ONE pack, one pack leader, and all animals are ranked second in that pack, even if those animals are merely visiting the house. To do this the owner must be aware of how to gain the respect of the dog. Without respect you cannot lead. No animal on the planet, including humans, follows if they don't respect. They don't respect if they don't trust. The building of the pack has begun and all behavior, rules and breakdowns will now stem from this one truism.

The second skill, then, that the owner must master is to gain the respect of the dog. Respect is engendered by demonstrating consistently, in a variety of situations and conditions, successful emotional, physical and psychological skills and the ability to enforce them. The owner must be able to stop the dog from testing other members of the pack. He must be able to administer discipline in such a manner and at such a level as to thoroughly communicate intolerance of unacceptable behavior. He must be able to allocate, fairly, affection on a one-on-one basis while teaching other pack members to wait patiently for their turn. He must clearly communicate what the rules of the pack are and insist that they not be challenged. He must clearly communicate that he alone will determine the behavioral response of all under his command in any situation. Pressure to desist in engaging in undesirable behavior and activities must be exerted by the leader when the dog's response is not acceptable, and dissipation of pressure must occur when behavior is acceptable. The owner must be able to do all of this while, at the same time, adjusting to the individual temperaments and overall emotional fluctuations, without sacrificing the balance of the group. Not an easy thing for the owner.

In order to teach an owner how to gain respect, one must also teach the owner how dogs think and what skills they measure in order to determine where to bestow that respect. It is then necessary to work with each owner to individually develop the consistency of communication and response that will spark respect in the dog. Each person communicates slightly differently as regards tone, emphasis, strength of displeasure and expectation of a desired response. Still, the communication exists and it is imperative for a trainer to develop this in the owner so that it is understood by the dog and so that the owner can read and understand when they are not communicating clearly. Owners must have the ability to move from emotional to psychological to physical displeasure/discipline at the dog's behavior in order to effectively communicate. After all, the dog has probably run through the same three levels in its misbehavior and to be unwilling to correctly discipline in the area the dog chooses to push is to ensure loss of respect. Only the weak back down from the challenge and in the dog's world, the weak are not respected, they are marginalized or killed. However, everyone has a different method of "drawing a line in the sand" and it is the trainer's responsibility to teach each human how to draw that line early and firmly and enforce it at the correct level. The majority of correction or discipline can be administered strictly by psychological or emotional pressure.

Think of it as if you were driving a car. In order to avoid a problem or accident from happening while driving you apply pressure to the brakes. To continue on your way, you release the pressure, you take your foot off the brake. You don't need to come to a full stop every time you see a potential problem, you simply correct and continue. It is the same when applying pressure to dogs; the psychological and emotional pressures are your brakes.

Problem Two can have a complication. Should the group be composed of more than one dog, the average owner will not truly be considered leader as, in all probability, the dogs have paired up and bonded and the human is looked on as a supply-line of weak and limited means and a sub-pack to them.

It is imperative that a trainer be able

to teach the owner how to separate the dogs emotionally and establish a bonding situation between each dog and himself. Without this, the dogs will ignore the human when and wherever they chose to, and do as they wish in tandem. New and old conventional obedience methods simply do not work in this kind of situation as the dogs don't consider the human relevant, for the most part, in their world.

Many trainers do not seem to be able to identify this dog-on-dog bond and do not teach owners about it in order to forestall behavioral problems. The owner is continuously faced with this serious and subversive relationship between the dogs and is not aware of it and has no skills with which to alter it. The trainer is in the dark about it. The dogs are in control and make their own rules without negative results – until such time as they ignore a command and run out into the road and one gets killed.

Finally, it is necessary to teach owners how to have a relationship with their dog. I realize this sounds odd, but it's true. Owners will be all over the place in dealing with their dog. Verbally, they'll sound as if they're trying out for Nazi command boot camp. They'll bark orders at the dog, tell it every little thing it may do, and put a full stop to any wayward, or even suspicious, behavior. (This last indicates there is no trust in their dog or his responses.) Emotionally, they'll love the dog up, and then become afraid or insecure when the safety of the house walls, the yard fence or the leash is not there. They'll project fear when being approached by other dogs or people. They'll be harsh in their commands, but hyper in tone of voice in their "good dog." In the world of people, this extreme of emotion is labeled manic. But, we flood our dogs with this constantly. Finally, physically we will correct before error (pop the leash and then give the command), restrain the dog before letting it make an error to learn from, and stop the dog from engaging in life in order to have and/or maintain control.

It's hard to generalize what makes a relationship as each combination of dog/person is unique. I almost always have to deal with the duo to help the human succeed at the relationship, improve his confidence and then I need only talk to him about what he could do to improve it. Once a human has a successful relationship with a dog, he gains confidence, relaxes and deals with the next dog better and more quickly. Often it is only a matter of small suggestions or tweaking to aid the person with a new dog, not the large overhaul that was required with the first animal. Each new dog in that person's life benefits from the owner's previous dog/human relationships. Each new dog is often thought by the owner to be "the best dog" he's had. In a sense this is true as each new dog reflects the improvement of you, the owner.

Chapter

8

Group Therapy

The hand holding the pen was dragged across the check and whipped along the tabletop and the harried woman made a disgusted hiss. Struggling with her dog's leash, she reeled the very excited, intent and straining Springer-cross close to her side. She gave a small, rueful smile and began to write a new check.

Tearing it from her checkbook she attempted to hand it over as the Springer renewed its tugging on the leash. The woman's hand jerked and danced as the volunteer vainly tried to catch hold of the moving check, only to have it repeatedly snatched from her reach at the last second.

After three or four attempts to transfer her payment, the woman grabbed her dog's collar firmly and placed the check on the table and slid it with one finger to the waiting volunteer. Keeping a firm hold on her dog, she quickly moved away toward the chairs.

A very tall, slim, elegantly dressed woman in a pair of khaki, tailored pants and deep, berry-colored cashmere sweater stepped up and placed a small, nylon-mesh, soft-sided crate, with the name "Contessa" prominently embroidered on its side, on the table. From its depth came a high-pitched sound that wavered between a despairing yodel and a scream of indignation. The lady's cheek showed a small tic at the ear-piercing wail which emanated from the carrier next to her.

"Tinkerbell in a frustrated rage," JoAnn, the clinic organizer whispered. I laughed.

A small Bichon was next, relaxing between its owner's legs and attempting to stay out of the increasing commotion, watching curiously as the line behind it grew and become more active.

I stood at the front of the room and eyed all the dogs in their various stages of inappropriate behavior, when suddenly a tall man stepped up to the registration table with a hound that gave every indication that it would provoke a serious wreck if his actions weren't halted immediately.

The shelter people and I had discussed this exact scenario the day before and had reviewed plans on how to handle just such an event.

Often the owners were unaware of what, exactly, their dogs were doing. They wrote-off the actions of their pets as excited and happy to be at the clinic, when in reality some of the dogs were bullies and head-hunting for a victim. The timid or frightened dogs were the easiest targets and often bore the brunt of these emotional and physical blitzkriegs.

In this case, however, it was much worse. The hound was malevolently keying in on a German shepherd mix about three places back, which was displaying much the same attitude, and the two dogs had locked eyes. It was only a matter of time before the two boys decided to compare testosterone levels.

"Patty," my voice conveyed my warning and I motioned to the hound.

Patty stepped up with a tact and diplomacy that often escaped me and quietly offered to hold the big dog for the man while he signed in. She artfully moved the tensing hound away from the group of waiting dogs and made him sit down.

The shelter personnel, as one, silently released a sigh and returned to their duties. I continued revicwing the dogs entering the room. All of them would be staying for the full-day portion of the clinic and engaging in behavioral-obedience that afternoon and this was my opportunity to see them at their worst.

The owners were nervous and unsure, which caused the dogs to exhibit every behavior under the sun, and because the owners didn't trust their dogs, they spread throughout the room picking seats some distance from each other.

There were thirty dogs signed up for the full-day portion of the clinic and another forty-nine morning seminar attendees. The shelter would make good money from this fund-raiser. I was happy.

I checked the clock, saw that with only a single exception, everyone had found a seat and I determined it was time to begin.

"Hi. I'm Susan O..." an electric screech from the center of the audience brought me to a halt. The heads nearest the lady bearing Contessa swiveled to stare in her direction. Her faced colored to match her sweater and she "shushed" at the crate on the chair beside her. The dog fell silent.

"...Overfield. I'm glad to see you all..." a Valkyrie-like sound of rage brought the introduction to a halt again.

"Contessa, shush!" The woman keeping her face a blank mask, eyes firmly locked on me, and without any discernable movement of her mouth, sternly hissed the command. Immediately, the sound stopped.

"I want to welcome you all to the shelter's Psych-O..."

Contessa, with all the power her lungs could command, screamed a full-throated howl of thwarted rage worthy of a banshee. She violently thrashed around in the small fabric crate, causing it to bulge simultaneously on the sides and top and sent it skittering to the edge of the chair from which it threatened to topple.

The people on either side of the small dog surreptitiously inched their chairs away from this unexpected display of demonic possession. Their expressions ranged from disbelief to outright shock.

As the crate began to slip off the chair, the woman discarded all evidence of self-containment and made a mad lunge to catch it before it hit the floor. Contessa continued unabated with her mad contortions and vocal diatribe. Struggling with her composure and the crate, the woman kept her head bowed.

"...Psych-O Clinic. This morning we'll..."

With the mesh door firmly clamped in her teeth, Contessa proceeded to whip her head back and forth, while growling madly. The crate slid, slithered, jumped, and bounced as the poor woman attempted to keep secure hold on it and quiet the dog within. I could feel her radiating acute embarrassment.

Dogs throughout the room were now fixated on the action taking place in the fourth row. Some had their heads cocked in interest. The hound was whining and giving every indication that he was getting ready to rush over and become involved. One relatively young Australian shepherd was trying to bury its head under its owner's sweater.

Abandoning all thoughts of a formal welcome I stepped into the audience, smiled reassuringly, and relieved the woman of the still-writhing Contessa. Returning to the front I plopped the crate on the table next to me, unzipped its door, and made the small hellion wait to be allowed out.

Contessa was a Havanese-mix. She couldn't have weighed much more than ten pounds, but her determination to have it her way was immeasurable. She was an incredibly smart dog and it took her a very short time to come to the conclusion that the odds were not in her favor this time. She instantly became quiet and sat when told.

It was during this unexpected demonstration that I saw from the corner of my eye a golden retriever that was having a melt down. It had been unwilling to sit and be calm since the moment he had entered the building. The golden was on a retractable leash – which I really detest – and they are the only thing I suggest owners replace in the way of dog-related equipment. (They are only useful for dogs so old that their greatest excitement is breathing. Retractable leashes allow the dog to learn bad habits and behaviors and offer no control to the owner.) The big dog had paced, wriggled, wiggled, scooted, and pranced under and around the chair on the long lead, until the owner was tied to her seat. If I'd only had a camera....

The golden's owner was vainly attempting to extricate herself from her bondage as the dog poked a nose in her face, gave her long, loving licks, nudged her hands, dashed off, almost pulled the chair over, and generally misbehaved.

Giving a warning sound and look to Contessa, I dropped her leash and made my way to the distressed and trussed woman. I quickly caught hold of her retriever's collar, unclipped the useless leash and replaced it with the spare I carried in my back pocket and handed it over, leaving her to untangle the retractable at her leisure.

As I straightened I caught sight of the big hound in the back engaged in covert terrorism while his owner stood oblivious to his actions.

By means of intense looks and emotional and psychological pressure, the muscular dog had forced a Chocolate Lab to seek shelter under its owner's chair. The poor Lab was stressed, frightened and cowering while the hound continuously inched forward toward its intended victim.

"Sir," I caught the hound owner's attention, "Please make your dog sit."

"He's not doing anything."

"Yes, sir, he is. He's putting pressure on that Lab."

"He's not doing anything." The man's reply was curt and challenging.

Here was a perfect example of an owner unaware of his dog's behavior, what the dog was communicating, how it was affecting the other dogs around it and unwilling to accept what was being pointed out to him. I intended to use it as a teaching tool.

"Sir, your dog is flying beneath the radar and while he's not doing anything overt, or that you consider bad behavior, he IS causing that Lab a lot of stress. Your dog is communicating in a very clear manner exactly what he intends to do. And the Lab is not happy."

"Henry has not even touched that lab." He replied testily and with resentment now that the room was looking in his direction.

"Henry doesn't need to touch the Lab. Dogs don't use verbal communication; they use emotional, body language and visual communication. He is clearly having an unpleasant conversation with that Lab and the Lab is miserable. You need to make Henry return to your side and stay there on a sit." My tone had elevated to brooking no argument.

During this entire acrimonious interplay another dog, just a few feet away, had repeatedly jumped to its feet and deafened the room with a barrage of barking.

Without a thought to the still-sitting Contessa I walked to the back of the room, took the leash of the barking dog and brought it back up front with me. I gave the correction sound and insisted the dog be quiet and sit. Being the basically good dog that it was, it did it without an argument. Silence had been restored. I soon returned it to its owner.

During the next thirty minutes of discussing the behavior of the four dogs I had just gotten under control, I discovered many things, though none of them surprised me.

The hound and barking dog were both in the same family – go figure. This couple did not tell their dogs that their behavior was wrong unless the behavior was egregious, (biting, running off, not coming) to them as humans. Still, the pair had come to the clinic as their dogs had behavior problems. The couple volunteered at another town's shelter and thought it "mean" to restrict any dog from having freedom and interacting as it wished with other dogs. Unless, of course, the dog was aggressive, then it shouldn't be allowed out in public.

The golden was a rescue and the woman made every excuse under the sun for its shortcomings because of its background. In her mind, allowing the dog freedom and unconditional love was making up for its poor previous life. But now the dog's behavior had deteriorated so much and was causing such problems she was forced to seek a remedy. She wanted a fix, but not if it meant she had to be "mean."

Contessa's owner admitted freely that the small dog was spoiled and got her way in everything. She didn't know how to regain the upper hand and their relationship was an ongoing argument. One she rarely won.

As we discussed dogs, the way they learned, what they thought, how they interacted, a hand crept into the air.

"I'm Jane. I've tried to come to your last two clinics, but I wasn't able to catch Griz."

I was so glad to see this woman. I had spoken on the phone several times with her and she had a real problem dog that I knew we could help.

Griz had been rescued from a very bad situation and was consumed by terror. When Jane had gotten him home she had let him out in the back yard. He had run from her and spent the next few months "ghosting" (a term I use to denote a dog or person you know is there, but cannot be seen) and couldn't even be coerced into the house. The only way she knew he was still in the yard was by the daily disappearance of his food.

Twice she had signed up for a clinic and twice she had been unable to catch Griz. She had owned him for about a year and, this time, with the help of a friend she managed to catch him and put him in the car. He was so stressed at this that he was sick several times on the way to the clinic.

He now remained under her chair, silent, terrified, curled and unmoving. He had dived under there the second she sat down and had not moved in two hours.

It was painful to see a dog in that much distress. To be living with that much fear and insecurity. Especially when I knew we could change it and offer Griz the world.

"I've tried everything I can think of to convince Griz I want to be friends. I try to offer him treats. He won't let me pet him, though I can touch him with my foot if he's not aware it will happen. But, the second he knows I'm doing it, he bolts. I'm patient with him and try to talk nicely so he won't be afraid, but he won't come near me. I can't walk him. I can't love him. I can't seem to reach him. How does a person fix that?"

This woman had all the good intentions in the world and was doing everything wrong. She'd read the books and watched the videos. Nothing made a difference.

"Jane...imagine yourself in a dark alley. An unknown man approaches and tries to sweet talk you with promises of candy. He's pushy about being friends. He never stops trying to convince you to come to him. Do you trust him and his motives?"

"No." It was an epiphany for her.

"Of course not, anything or anyone that tries that hard has to have an ulterior motive and you feel it's probably not in your best interest to help them achieve it." I smiled.

"We humans know this at an atavistic level. We simply fail to apply it to other animals. We know we don't want to hurt the dog. Still we behave in exactly the wrong way and communicate something entirely different without meaning to." I walked to where she was sitting.

Taking Griz's leash from her I unemotionally led the resisting dog from beneath the chair and returned to the front of the room.

I continued to finish out the morning session with Griz at my side. I didn't bother to look at him, talk to him, pet him, yet neither did I allow him to leave or break a sit. When he rose from his place I simply cleared my throat and he immediately returned to a sit. For close to forty minutes Griz and I were inseparable. Then the morning ended and it was time for lunch. I kept Griz with me as people left for the lunch or to go home. Some came up to speak with me and still I held Griz at my side.

Finally the only people remaining in the room were me; the clinic organizer, JoAnn; her co-organizer, Katherine; Griz, Jane and Jane's friend.

"Hold lunch for me," I begged JoAnn and Katherine. "Jane, let's walk." Griz and I led the way from the building. He flowed beside me, he held his head up and looked at the world, much of his anxiety had left him and he was a happier dog. We didn't go far, just out to the parking lot where I turned over the leash to Jane.

"Stop begging him to be your friend. Be confident. Show him you have the world under control. That will do more to help him than anything."

She was thunderstruck and at a loss for words. The change in the dog was so sudden and diametrically opposed to his earlier demeanor.

"I'll see you after lunch. Go relax." I smiled and headed off to eat.

The morning had gone well and I was satisfied. The shelter would make good money on the one-day fund-raiser and that was important to me. It had been a struggle to get the clinics to be accepted as a viable method to help dogs. It had been an even bigger struggle to get the shelters to offer one.

This particular shelter had a Board member who had used my methods on all of her own, plus several shelter dogs. She suggested to the shelter director that it would be a good educational program for the public and profitable fund-raising opportunity for the shelter.

The director had asked me to visit the shelter and then cold-picked several dogs for me to work in order to assess the value of what I offered. He had been impressed at the speed with which the dogs responded to this particular method of handling and had agreed, on the spot, that it would be beneficial to offer a clinic.

He and I had discussed at length why other shelters didn't pick up on offering the clinics. Most of them had a pat response that "their trainer wouldn't like it". I simply couldn't understand what the feelings of a trainer had to do with helping owners improve their skills and offering the general public some education about dogs with the added bonus of raising much-needed funds for the shelters.

In my state of Montana, three shelters had capitulated and offered the clinics. The public response had been overwhelmingly positive and owners, who came from all over the state, were extremely pleased with the behavioral and obedience changes in their dogs.

Still, the majority of the shelters wouldn't sponsor a clinic for fear of insulting their trainers or they simply didn't believe the method was legitimate. This shelter was offering its third clinic and each successive clinic had garnered more participants and raised more funds.

I returned from lunch and was immediately descended upon by owners who had questions, wished to tell me of the difference in their dog's behavior already, or merely wanted to talk about dogs.

This always happened and I allowed about ten minutes of this much-needed conversation before beginning the afternoon's work.

Looking around the room I mentally checked off the heads of three different rescue groups, all from out-of-state, representatives from two shelters, several dog-foster individuals; the remainder were simply owners with their dogs, some having come from neighboring states.

It was certainly a mixed-bag. There

was a Border collie pup, the hound, a beagle, the Aussie, a Great Dane, a greyhound, the Havanese-mix, two Labs, a Lab-mix, a German shepherd mix, a young Rottweiller, an Akita, a dachshund, a springer, a Bichon, a golden retriever, and everything in between.

We got down to business. Taking everything we'd talked about during the morning, we began to apply it to obedience in the afternoon. Within just a few minutes most of the dogs were working off-leash for me and the owners were astounded.

By mid-afternoon we'd moved outside and solved many problems. Dogs were now sitting and staying in place, their behavior was such that they no longer bothered other dogs around them. We worked on walking nicely on the leash, then off-leash.

During this period I had one woman that I struggled to reach. Sondra had driven through three states with her friend, Sue, and a rescue dog, Campo, that had come close to biting several people. Nothing I said or did seemed to make her realize that the dog was reflecting her intense fear. She kept it on a tight leash and far from the others in the clinic.

I finally decided it was time to make her step up and work on her problem. Approaching the pair I watched her fear increase dramatically, which in turn caused the poor dog to morph from moderately-stressed to outright terror.

As I stood by Campo, I kept my eyes averted so as not to place undue pressure on him, and attempted to talk Sondra down to a reasonable level of quietude. As I reached over for the leash the dog reached critical mass and lost it. Hurling itself around, it lunged, whipped back and forth and sank its teeth into my leg, then ricocheted off in another direction as it mindlessly struggled to run from the intolerable situation.

Sondra became terrified and the dog, its eyes glazed in hysteria, increased its fight against the thin restraint and the avalanche of emotion flowing from the woman who was now frozen in spot.

Ruefully I looked down at my jeans. There were four clear holes where the dog had bitten me and a spreading circle of blood. The swelling was already evident. So much for my new jeans.

"Here, Sue, take the leash."

Sue was a veteran dog handler and had rescued many dogs. Her calm, confident manner was instantly communicated and easily read by the dogs and was much needed at this moment.

Sondra was in such a state that she didn't seem to hear me. Dog and human shared the brain-freeze which made it impossible to communicate with them.

Sue and I made eye contact and she reached over and smoothly took control of the hysterical dog. Without a word she pulled the dog to her side and we gave it time to begin to regain self-control. Campo's eyes slowly came back into focus, he managed to follow the sit command and his breathing slowed; all the while I was calming Sondra.

It had been a spectacular display and I turned to find the entire roster of the clinic, both dogs and humans, frozen in spot. Telling everyone to hang on, I went inside to perform triage on my leg.

I was rarely injured in the course of work, though it was always a possibility with certain dogs. I never entertained the odds, merely continued on with the job at hand.

Peeling my pants off, I couldn't remember the last time I'd been bitten. It was while soaping the area just above my knee that it came to me; ten years ago. That encounter had almost cost a finger.

Floating up from my subconscious came numerous encounters over that span in which I'd had some close calls, but none had resulted in being bitten. A knock on the bathroom door brought me back to the present.

"Come in."

The door opened and Katherine's head popped into view.

"Do you need...Oh my gosh! Do you want to go to the hospital?" Katherine's

face had paled to a ghostly shade of white.
I looked down at my leg with fresh
eyes. It was swollen, had three deep punc-
tures and a gash which was seeping blood
and was already exhibiting shades of blue,
red and purple.

"No, thanks. Can you get me an ice
pack and an ace bandage?"

"Sure. Oh, geez! Does it hurt?"
Katherine disappeared without waiting for
my answer. In a very short time she was
back.

Try as I might I couldn't strap the ice
pack under my jeans. I had to be content
with anchoring it over the hole the dog had
created in my pants. I didn't like this as it
would be a constant reminder to people of
the bite. They would react differently to the
dog and that was the last thing it needed.

After ensuring the pack would stay in
place, I went outside to address the group.
It was important that they understand that
the dog was not aggressive, but out of its
mind with fear. I also needed to impress
upon Sondra that I was not going to go to
the ER and the dog was not going to be re-
ported.

The dog was here to have this problem fixed. If I kicked it out of the clinic
due to this incident, then how could it be
helped?

Sue still maintained control of Campo who had calmed considerably and I ges-

tured her forward into the waiting group
and we got on with life and the clinic. Sondra, an emotional mess, remained just outside the group's periphery, silently watching. The dog, however, in Sue's competent,
calm hands behaved entirely differently and
was less stressed.

Now in the large park-like setting
attached to the building we ran the dogs
through their paces once again. I quickly
assessed each dog and then concentrated
on its owner.

The dogs knew what to do and understood what was expected. The owners,
however, had shown a dramatic drop in self-
confidence now that they were outside and
didn't have walls to ensure their dog didn't
run off. The beautiful, wide-open tract of
grass only struck fear into their hearts. A
few of the dogs were taking advantage of
their owner's hesitancy.

As my gaze flitted across the group
they came to settle on a silent battle of wills
not ten feet from me. I watched as the ti-
tanic struggle continued and had to laugh.
Finally, I crossed to the oddly matched pair
and intervened.

Michael was a big, beefy man weighing around 280 pounds, with a barrel chest,
a deep, warm voice, and arms the size of
small tree trunks. He stood about six-and-
a-half feet tall and his smile was a joy to be-
hold. He was relaxed, self-confident, funny

and friendly. He made one feel as if she'd just met Santa in the off-season.

Hans, the love of Michael's life, was a long-haired dachshund weighing, roughly, eight pounds. He was joyful, of good temperament, friendly to all, and when he ran, even his long ears (sailing in the wind he'd created), radiated happiness. To watch this dog was to watch unabashed ecstasy. It was impossible not to smile around Hans, even when he misbehaved.

But, Hans was smart. He was cunning. He was determined. He was winning. Michael was at a loss as to how to get the small dachsie under control. Hans exploited this shamelessly.

When Michael gave a command, Hans would look at him and then gravely turn away to pursue his own agenda. If Michael told Hans to "come," the pup would sit down and stare unblinkingly until Michael approached to catch him. Then, with surprising swiftness, the young dachsie would nimbly scoot away and laughingly begin the game of "catch-me-if-you-can." It was premeditated, it was superbly executed, it was funny to watch. But, it was no longer endearing as Hans, just three weeks earlier, had dashed into the street and had narrowly missed being killed by a car. Michael had been terrified by the near-miss and was determined to ensure it never happened again.

I worked Hans for a time and soon the young dog realized he faced insurmountable odds and, with great good grace, gave in and began to come each and every time he was given the command.

Michael took a stab at getting Hans to come and pleasure oozed from his every pore when the tiny dog trotted to him and sat. He couldn't contain himself and knelt down to share his happiness with his best friend.

Hans tilted his head up at the big man and his look conveyed his thought. "If this is all you wanted, why didn't you say so in the first place?" I grinned and left the two to work on it a little longer.

I wended my way between the different dogs and stopped at the side of Mark and Speed. Mark was the head of a breed rescue group from another state and Speed was the bane of his existence.

Speed, a classic Gordon setter, had been with two families prior to being shunted into the rescue. He walked well on the leash, sat nicely, greeted all people politely; in short, he was well-behaved. But, the second he was off-leash he was the living embodiment of the dog in the Chevy Chase movie, "Funny Farm." He was gone.

He ran. He ran so far and so often the dog had frequent flier miles. He could disappear faster than Houdini. He would be miles away in the time it took to grab your coat.

The last time this had happened Mark had been showing him off to potential adopters. He had taken Speed outside to let the couple walk and play with him and Speed had managed to get loose and shot off for a romp through the countryside. It had taken six hours to catch him. Needless to say, the couple had declined to adopt Speed.

Even Mark was at the end with the lithe dog. Speed had been with him for almost a year now and he knew this problem had to be solved or he'd never find a home for the wonderful dog. He'd spent too many hours trailing him uphill and down dale to kid himself about Speed's chances with a normal family if this problem persisted.

I measured both man and dog with a glance. Speed was relaxed, listening, and doing well. Mark had a death-grip on the leash and was unwilling to give the slightest freedom to him.

"Mark, drop the leash and walk Speed over there and back, please."

The man suffered a spasm right in front of me. His eyes opened wide, his hand tightened on the leash and his shoulders hunched. His jaw clenched and a vein popped out on his neck and throbbed rapidly. He held my gaze with the stricken look of one who's just been informed that they have been chosen as the next sacrificial victim.

"C'mon, Susan, he'll be history. Speed'll take off and we won't catch him." Desperation tinged every word.

Speed raised his chin, cocked his head to the right, and one ear came forward in interest as he absorbed the melt-down of the human at his side.

Reaching out I pried Mark's fingers from around the leash and walked off with Speed. After a few feet I calmly dropped the leash to the ground and the two of us continued without a hitch. Speed and I walked this way for about five minutes and returned to Mark. Stopping in front of the stunned man, Speed instantly sat and waited patiently.

"Mark, take Speed for a walk. And don't forget to drop the leash."

With great hesitancy Mark reached for the leash. I realized if I didn't get him in the right frame of mind, Speed would make his worst fears come true.

For the next few minutes I worked on helping Mark rebuild confidence and communication before I allowed him to begin the walk. Then I sent the two of them off. Mark was stiff and unsure as he started away and I stopped him.

"Zen dog walking, Mark." I gave his shoulders a short massage, told him to take a deep breath and let go, then with a little shove between his shoulder blades sent him on his way.

The transformation was immediate and obvious. The longer Mark and Speed walked the better they did. Pleasure and confidence was apparent as they made their way back to me. "That was fantastic!" Mark was elated.

"That was to be expected." I said. "We've spent this afternoon building up to that. You should be able to do that most of the time. Speed may make a mistake, but if you're paying attention, he probably won't be able to take off any longer."

Mark's enthusiasm knew no bounds. Speed, on the other hand, was more contained and made do with two thumps of his tail on the ground.

The dog caught my attention and I could read his thoughts, "Special needs owners. You must have patience." I smiled at Speed and was rewarded with faster tail thumping.

By the end of the clinic almost everyone was scattered hither and yon working with their dogs off-leash. The exception was Sondra, whom I was unable to reach and convince to let go of her fear. Still, she had made great strides and she and the dog had, for a short time, worked together close by other dogs and people. That, in itself, was a huge improvement considering that prior to the clinic she'd stopped taking the dog out in public for fear of it biting. Still, I wanted her to understand what Campo was capable of and I had her pass the dog to her friend.

Under Sue's calm direction, Campo joined the group. His leash was dropped and he ignored the other dogs and humans. I wanted, with this demonstration, to convince Sondra that the problem lay not with Campo, but her own emotional state. She was the source of Campo's problem and she needed to resolve her fear in order to handle the dog. Sue promised she would remain available for moral support and guidance and that gave me hope. I wanted this improvement to continue so both Sondra and the dog would benefit.

Griz, once so fearful, had done extremely well. He had a way to go, but he had walked at Jane's side and actually sought out contact with her by the end of the day. It was a first for him and very important and reaffirming for Jane. I felt they would do well together.

Contessa had transformed into the model of demure deportment and regally sat at her mistress's side. I voiced a warning, however, that the small dog would push the limits several more times before truly accepting her owner as the supreme leader. Even at the end of this long day, Contessa's owner was still elegant, without a smudge of dirt or hair out of place. The tic had vanished and been replaced with certitude and confidence, so I knew it would be alright.

Michael had removed Han's leash about mid-afternoon and hadn't bothered to reattach it. As if they had been doing this together for years, he and the small dog were totally in synch and content.

I gathered all the participants together and had each of them walk his dog, off-leash, in front of the group one last time. Support, pride and pleasure radiated from the watching people. The dogs responded to the happiness and applause of the humans around them and walked with a bounce in their step. The owners could barely contain themselves.

We ended on this high note. I reminded the group how far they'd come in only four or five hours of work and that, if they continued to build on what we'd begun, it would only improve. I reminded them that they could contact me anytime, about anything.

As usual, it took almost an hour for me to get away. Owners needed and wanted to talk, to express their pleasure, their pride, their amazement. They wanted to recount horror stories of other obedience classes and how this clinic had been so different and how much it meant to them. I listened patiently, but finally had to break away.

As I pulled out of the parking lot I

grabbed my cell phone and speed dialed a friend who was a doctor.

"Could you order up some broad-spectrum antibiotic, I was bitten by a dog at the clinic today."

"Sure. But, before I do, I have a question about my dog, Bob..."

All the dogs, various breeds & ages

Every dog which attended this clinic arrived with behavioral issues. The majority had already been through another obedience class and the issues remained. In some cases, they had even increase in severity.

The problems varied from benign (not walking well on a leash), to frightening and potentially dangerous, such as acting aggressively toward dogs or people.

The dogs in this clinic were in no way exceptionally high-risk, though for a few cases their problems were severe and posed a myriad of risks for both themselves and their owners.

The dogs could not be successfully trained without training the owner. The clinic offered that training. Each and every dog attending the clinic showed behavioral changes in a very short time. This allowed the owners to see what their dog could accomplish and gave the person the incentive to learn how to communicate with their companion. It was easy to learn, common sense, and the humans left with the ability to successfully continue making a new skill into a behavioral habit.

The greatest surprise of all to the participating owners was that their dog functioned, along with all the others, together as a group off-leash by the end of the day. That was a wondrous moment for them.

Owners finished the day with a greater understanding of their dog, what it took and how to communicate correctly and effectively, and how to successfully create good behavioral patterns in their companions. Both dogs and humans were happier.

Questions & Answers

Q: "Is it really possible to learn and/or teach my dog anything in a one-day clinic? Does the clinic format really work? Both my obedience trainer and a friend say it's a scam. Is it? Your testimonial page and the newspaper article don't seem to think so."

A: It is often thought, and said, that one cannot train a dog in a single day. To some extent this is true. You cannot make new behaviors become habit in a single day. You can, however, train for a new behavior in an extremely short time.

It is also said you cannot train five, ten, or thirty dogs in one day and that this means the clinics won't work. This is not true at all. Those that say this usually cannot train one dog in a day and, therefore, can't comprehend the possibility of ten, much less thirty.

With very few exceptions, and these are usually predicated on the owner's abilities, all dogs which attend clinics respond well and quickly to this behavioral training. It is the way dogs inherently behave and the means by which they, themselves, train other dogs and so they can understand, immediately, what is being required of them.

All dogs can be trained in this manner with the rare exception of the dog which is suffering an inherent health or idiopathic disease or problem, and this is a very small number. Some learn quickly, some take more time. But, all can be trained.

The truly aggressive dog is not as prevalent as people are led to believe. They are out there, and because of the severity of their behavioral problems must be dealt with on a one-on-one basis for a variety of reasons: safety for others, intensity of training, education of the owner; and trainer concentration, before they are capable of entering the more mainstream group of the clinic.

But it all comes down to training the owner to communicate correctly. This is what takes the greatest effort and amount of time.

As there are only a finite number of people who simply cannot communicate with their pet, the clinic teaches owners how best to communicate with their dog.

This method is easily accessible and understandable to the owner, they are willing and able to implement it and they then experience success. (It is often the owner who determines how long it takes a dog to learn this method.)

This is where the majority of trainers and methods fail. They blame the owner and/or dog for not mastering what they are teaching.

Occasionally a person attends a clinic and simply will not accept what is being taught. There are any number of different reasons for this. Everything they see, hear and do that day flies in the face of what they believe is right for dogs. These individuals cannot and will not change. Their dogs will evidence the ability to successfully follow a variety of commands, but the owner is unwilling to change so nothing can be achieved for the dog.

However, owners want something better for their dogs and the clinics supply that. These people like the fact that the clinic, often times, is also raising funds for good causes. It's a win-win-win situation.

Owners frequently have concerns as to how they will handle the unexpected after the clinic is finished. For this reason I always reassure them that they may call or e-mail with any questions. They should пot hesitate to contact me. This gives them a boost of confidence and psychologically helps them overcome many hurdles that they might face.

For the few who contact me, their questions are often banal and result from their second-guessing themselves since it takes time for them to shed the old human-based information they learned from other training methods.

Can you learn this method in a day?
　Yes.
Can the dog learn it in less than a day?
　Yes.
Can you maintain the level of good behavior with only one day of instruction?
　Yes.
Can you be a better, more secure, relaxed and confident leader to your dog?
　Yes.
Can you and your dog have a better, more enjoyable relationship?
　Yes.
Can you improve the quality of your dog's life by attending a clinic?
　Yes.
Does the clinic format really work?
　Yes, and the dogs are living proof of that.

Acknowledgements

No one ever, truly, does anything on their own. This book could never have been completed without the help of many, many people—and dogs.

Every single dog in these stories, and a greater number that never made the pages of this book, are to be thanked for helping me learn to communicate with their owners.

I wish to thank the large number of clients, who have become fast friends, who pushed, badgered, and repeatedly insisted that I needed to write this.

Then there are the individuals who unstintingly gave their support, help, advice, time, talent, and belief in this method, in order to ensure this book reached your hands. Thank you is simply not adequate to express how much I value each and every one you.

Ric Valois, who understood exactly what I was attempting to explain and often pushed me to a simpler, clearer explanation that owners could grasp. He believed, he supported, and he was unwavering in his conviction that this was possible. And he loved me even when I became a pain about all of this.

Pam Hendrickson, each and every day becomes a more competent dog handler, and that insight made her comments about what I wrote that much more important. She was able to perform the unique job of editor, while not losing the core ideas of this method and how best to communicate them to the reader.

Ray and Diana Goff, of Amavi Cellars, are my great friends and the proud owners of the dog on the cover, Hagrid, who was trained from a pup in this method. Hagrid is famous and loved in the wine country, as well as being the "founding" winery dog of Washington. His picture can also be found in *The Winery Dogs of Walla Walla*.

Ruth Bell who carved out time from her hectic schedule, before trekking off to the Antarctic, to proof read this book several times.

Christian Cornelius who cheerfully undertook the thankless task of checking my erratic punctuation and, being the nice person she is, used pink, not red ink to make the notations.

I want to thank Matt Hocevar who created the cover. And re-created, and re-created, and re-created – and did it all with great creativity and patience.

And last, but most definitely NOT least, is Newt. For twelve long years he's been at my side. He's worked with me on livestock and saved me from myself many times. He has helped me to help many dogs come back from the edge and to teach owners what it can be like to have a real relationship with a great dog. It has been a relationship without leashes, without collars, and filled with mutual respect and love. It is the relationship that owners dream about and wish for, and I'm lucky enough to experience. He is the standard I hold all my dogs to and I am blessed that we are a team.

About the Author

Susan Overfield lives on 40 acres "out beyond God" in Montana. Her children are grown, but return home often, mainly to borrow things or drop their dogs off so they can go on vacation.

For over 35 years, Susan has taught dog owners about the physical & psychological well-being of their dogs, and pups, ages 8 weeks & older. Her unique, ground-breaking method—created for the average person—teaches dog psychology & behavior so that owners may be more successful, confident partners to their dogs. The media has dubbed her "'Montana's dog doctor' as she often delivers a perfect—or at least improved—pooch with less than an hour of training." Susan shares her "dog whisperer" technique throughout the United States, showing owners how to utilize dog psychology to train their dogs without using choke chains, pinch collars or treats. Whether through a private in-home consultation, a Dog Camp, or a "Psych-O" Clinic, for fund-raisers or private groups, Susan's clients are advocates of her proven method. To read about her method and learn how you can arrange a clinic in your area, contact Susan Overfield at www.overfieldkennel.com.